# Improving Learning Transfer

# Improving Learning Transfer

## A Guide to Getting More Out of What You Put Into Your Training

CYRIL KIRWAN

Routledge
Taylor & Francis Group

LONDON AND NEW YORK

First published in paperback 2024

First published 2009 by Gower Publishing

Published 2016 by Routledge
4 Park Square, Milton Park, Abingdon, Oxon OX14 4RN

and by Routledge
605 Third Avenue, New York, NY 10158

*Routledge is an imprint of the Taylor & Francis Group, an informa business*

**British Library Cataloguing in Publication Data**
Kirwan, Cyril
  Improving learning transfer : a guide to getting more out
  of what you put into your training
  1. Employees – Training of
  I. Title
  658.3'124

**Library of Congress Cataloging-in-Publication Data**
Kirwan, Cyril.
  Improving learning transfer : a guide to getting more out of what you put into your training / by Cyril Kirwan.
    p. cm.
  Includes index.
  ISBN 978-0-566-08844-5
  1. Organizational learning. 2. Employees--Training of. I. Title.

  HD58.82.K57 2008
  658.3'124--dc22

                                                                    2008036214

  ISBN : 978-0-566-08844-5 (hbk)
  ISBN : 978-1-03-283812-0 (pbk)
  ISBN : 978-1-315-58806-3 (ebk)

DOI: 10.4324/9781315588063

# Contents

# List of Figures

# List of Tables

# Introduction

## Setting the Scene

In today's constantly changing business environment, capable people are crucial to the success of organizations. To begin with, effective management is regularly cited as a major factor in gaining and sustaining competitive advantage. In addition, most of the approaches in the strategy literature such as innovation, learning and in particular leadership have at their core a need for managers who understand markets and challenges and have the ability to mobilize their workforces in pursuit of that advantage. They must achieve this against a background of continuous change, ever-intensifying competition, and a consequent need to maintain high levels of talent. Meanwhile, those whose levels of talent need to be maintained are also crucial to their organization's success. In order for them to contribute effectively, they must be enabled to develop the appropriate skills, knowledge and competence to carry out their job. This is even more important in today's knowledge organization, where a need for compliance with organizational rules and processes is gradually being replaced by a need to generate commitment to the organization's goals. In this regard, individuals at all levels still need to be, as Handy (1993) observed, obsessive about pursuing learning in order to keep up with the pace of change.

Furthermore, each year, billions of dollars, euro, pounds and yen (along with, increasingly, yuan and rupees) are spent in developing those capabilities through training, learning and development initiatives, as well as in other ways. Latest estimates from around the globe indicate that somewhere between two per cent and five per cent of organizations' payroll costs are spent on formal training. However, evidence concerning the value derived from what they spend on these interventions is not particularly encouraging. In so far as it can be measured, experts suggest that only somewhere between ten per cent (Broad and Newstrom 1992) and 34 per cent (Saks and Belcourt 2006) of skills and knowledge gained from training is still being applied by employees on-the-job a year later.

This latter fact is of major importance and the main reason for this book. Given the astronomical sums of money involved, closing the gap between what is invested and what is returned should be a priority for any organization. To do this requires a clear understanding of the factors that account for the gap. However, the complexity of the process of developing people (through training and development programmes as well as other interventions) does not make this understanding easy. Learning outcomes can be concerned with more than just imparting straightforward knowledge or simple skills. Programmes very often deal with more complex skills and may also be used as a way of changing attitudes. These outcomes are not easy to translate into improved on-the-job performance. Despite the difficulty in assessing the value of such interventions, there is however a strong need within organizations to at least attempt to do so, as would be the case with any other investment. In this regard, a growing number of organizations are applying (with varying degrees of success) return on investment or organizational impact methodologies. Whilst using these methodologies can provide useful information, that information is much less valuable if it does not take into account all of the factors that can affect application of new skills and knowledge on-the-job. In other words, there is a need for a clear understanding of the process of learning transfer. So, if organizations are to remain competitive, and develop the highly skilled people that will contribute to their future performance, improving learning transfer must receive more attention.

The book therefore aims to provide insight into a number of areas. Firstly, we'll look at what learning transfer actually is. Different perspectives on transfer will be offered, and a framework for understanding these perspectives will be provided. Next, we'll examine in more depth what those factors that affect learning transfer – in terms of trainee characteristics, training design factors and work environment characteristics – actually look like in practice, and what the training and development literature has to say about them. We'll look at how the factors exert their effect, which are the more important ones, how they interact with one another, and in doing so construct a workable learning transfer model for practitioners. Along the way we'll suggest what practical steps can be taken before, during and after training to improve the rate of transfer. Support for this will be provided by some real life case studies and scenarios that demonstrate the challenges in practice.

The material for this book comes from a number of sources. There is the author's own research, conducted over recent years, and his experience as a consultant in the area of training and development for the last 20 years. There is also the wisdom and experience of hundreds of managers, thinkers and researchers who, working on real issues with real people in real organizations over the last 50 years or so, have written up their work for others to learn from and develop. It is aimed primarily at those of you who have responsibility for management of the training, learning and development functions within your organization. It is intended to provide you with a comprehensive picture as to how you can make the most of your training and development efforts. For those of you whose responsibility it is to source training and development programmes, the book will provide a set of best practice guidelines against which can be measured the proposals of potential suppliers. Lastly, for those of you whose daily challenge as managers of people is to direct, monitor and reward the performance of those in your charge, it will give a valuable insight into what you can do to create the conditions where that can happen.

## References

Broad, M.L. and Newstrom, J. (1992). *Transfer of training: Action-packed strategies to ensure high payoff from training investments.* New York: Addison Wesley.

Handy, C. (1993). *Understanding organizations. 4th ed.* London: Penguin.

Saks, A.M. and Belcourt, M. (2006). An investigation of training activities and transfer of training in organizations. *Human Resource Management*, 45(4), 629–48.

# 1

# Learning and Learning Transfer

## Introduction

This chapter begins by setting the scene in terms of important learning concepts that have relevance for the application of learning in organizations. It also offers some definitions of learning transfer, as well as describing different types of transfer. Some distinctions are made between transfer of training and transfer of learning, as both terms appear regularly in the literature. Both behavioural and cognitive approaches are considered (don't worry, these will be explained!), and the relevance to transfer of adult learning principles, constructivist teaching methods and action learning are also dealt with. Those of you less theoretically-minded may prefer to skim over most of this chapter now and come back to it later. However you should make sure to have a look at the model that helps it all hang together before you leave the chapter.

## Defining Learning Transfer

Learning transfer, in the context of training and development activity, is discussed in the literature in terms of the generalization of material learned, such as skills acquired or knowledge gained in training back to the job, as well as maintenance of the learned material over a period of time on-the-job. One definition (Broad and Newstrom 1992, 5) describes it as 'the effective and continuing application, by trainees to their jobs, of the knowledge and skills gained in training – both on and off the job'. In effect, this means that trainees demonstrate their skills back on-the-job at least as well as they did at the end of training. Some others go further, and suggest that learning transfer also deals with whether or not learning in one situation will facilitate learning in subsequent similar situations (for example in learning Spanish if one already speaks French). In any event the definitions imply that learning is applied in the work situation, and that it is maintained up to a certain standard over time.

It is appropriate at this point to try and distinguish between training transfer and learning transfer. Some, for example Heisler and Benham (1992) contend that there has been a long-standing distinction in the field of human resource development between training and learning. They suggest that training is more immediate, practical and directed specifically at a task. On the other hand, they say, learning has a more long-term and academic focus. Others, such as Quinones and Ehrenstein (1996) also argue that training and learning are different, and describe training as a planned set of activities with cognitive, behavioural or affective change (thinking, behaving or feeling differently, that is, learning in one form or another) as one of its goals. Haskell (1998) echoes the above distinctions, and summarizes the argument by suggesting that learning tends to be more generative or creative than training, and results in a deeper level and a broader scope of transfer than does training, with a longer-term payoff.

Given the above descriptions, it seems that if learning is one of the goals of training, then it will also be one of the outcomes of effective training. Furthermore, learning is less likely to occur if some opportunity to try it out in practice doesn't occur, as proposed in models of learning such as that of Kolb (1984). As sustained on-the-job behaviour change is implied in the definitions of transfer above, it is very difficult to discuss transfer of training without discussing transfer of learning. Throughout this book, therefore, the term transfer of learning will be used.

## Types of Transfer

While there is a degree of overlap between different types of learning transfer, it is generally accepted that it can be categorized in terms of three dimensions. Firstly, in organizational training and development, perhaps the most common distinction is that between *near* and *far* transfer. Near transfer is quite specific and occurs mostly in situations where conditions in training are very similar to those in practice. The teaching of, for example, safety procedures, is intended to achieve near transfer only. On the other hand, these conditions would be different in the case of far (less specific) transfer. Applying management decision-making principles that were originally learned as part of an outdoor development programme involving crossing rivers or disposing of nuclear waste is an example of far transfer in operation. Secondly, another important distinction is that between *lateral* and *vertical* transfer. Vertical transfer is said to occur when a skill or piece of knowledge contributes directly to the acquisition of a wider skill or piece of knowledge. For example, a manager is likely to become confident more quickly in conducting an appraisal interview if they are already practised in giving performance feedback. Lateral transfer is more concerned with generalization over a broader set of situations at much the same level of complexity. In practice, negotiation skills learned for wage bargaining may also be useful for a procurement manager agreeing a price with a supplier. Thirdly, yet another distinction is made between *literal* and *figural* transfer. With literal transfer, what happens is that an intact skill or piece of knowledge is transferred to a new learning task. The negotiating skills example cited above is also a case of literal transfer. Figural transfer, on the other hand, involves using some part of what we already know in other fields as a way of thinking about a particular problem. A typical example, widespread within management, is the use of metaphors to explain concepts. Understanding behaviour in organizations using the 'organizational iceberg', or differentiating between 'mavericks' and 'cash cows' in terms of marketing strategy all operate by way of figural transfer.

Explanations for the different types of transfer have their roots in both behavioural and cognitive approaches to learning. Behaviourists take the view that an individual's observable and measurable behaviour should be the focus of attention, and as such concentrate on people's actions and their consequences. Thus in seeking to help a manager change their behaviour, for example, a coach using a behaviourist approach would emphasize ways of reinforcing desired behaviours (usually through rewards) and extinguishing undesired behaviours (usually through sanctions). On the other hand, cognitivists are more interested in the thinking, reasoning and self-talk behind the behaviour – in other words, what's going on inside the learner's head. A coach using more cognitive methods would be helping the individual identify *why* they behave in certain ways as a starting point for behaviour change. It's argued that behavioural approaches provide a reasonable explanation of literal transfer and near transfer, while the cognitive approaches are more satisfactory for explaining figural transfer and far transfer.

## Individual Learning

Work done by researchers from both the behavioural and the cognitive traditions has helped to provide the theoretical basis for much of the types of learning we see in organizations today. Whatever the foundations, however, there is broad agreement amongst researchers and training specialists that more experiential forms of learning are most suited to learning in organizations. This appears to be true whether the objectives of the learning intervention are to increase the level of knowledge or skill, change attitudes or change behaviour. For the acquisition of knowledge, early techniques such as programmed learning (built on the behaviourist approach) have given way to more experiential forms of learning (built on the cognitive approach). Experiential learning is also prevalent in interventions aimed at changing attitudes, as the research evidence indicates that attitudes developed through direct experience are stronger than those developed in other ways. The increasing use of action learning (which will be discussed more fully later), simulations and role playing are further examples of this development, using as they do techniques based on feedback, reflection and discussion of the learner's own experience.

The growth in the use of learning techniques just outlined may also have to do with what people are required to learn, particularly in management and other programmes concerned with the more complex skills and knowledge described earlier. The distinction between the 'deep' approach to learning, as opposed to the 'surface' approach (Marton and Saljo 1976) is one example. Deep learning activities are defined as those that maximize understanding, such as wide reading, discussion, theorizing, linking and hypothesizing. Surface learning approaches concentrate more on the literal – the lower order skills such as rote learning, describing and explaining. While inevitably learning interventions will require some surface learning (such as the use of mnemonics and acronyms for remembering procedures), people at higher levels in organizations are required to demonstrate more complex skills in areas such as analytical and conceptual thinking, handling motivation issues, dealing with resistance to change, and so on. Development and transfer of these sorts of skills, which is the focus of this book, is more likely to require a deep approach to learning.

## Constructivist Learning

The changes just described are at the heart of an increasingly popular approach to learning, known as the constructivist approach. Central to this approach is the idea that learners are encouraged to create their own meaning from the range of material and arguments with which they're presented. Constructivism asserts that learners bring to a learning intervention different personal knowledge and beliefs about 'how things are'. They are not 'empty vessels' waiting to be filled with new knowledge, and the knowledge they already have may be difficult to change. Dialogue is the starting point, and understanding occurs through question and explanation, through challenging, and through support and feedback. Intervention designs that promote constructivist learning will challenge learners to be more active, to interact with their peers, and to continually search to understand what they're learning. Indeed the same principles are also important in the context of 'adult' approaches to learning, and have important implications for learning transfer. These principles will be discussed further in Chapter 2.

## Action Learning

As discussed earlier, the growth in the adoption of adult learning principles and more constructivist teaching methods reflects a perceived need for a more active role for the learner in the process of learning, in order to enhance transfer. Another relevant development in this regard has been that of action learning. Interestingly, although action learning includes a number of the components mentioned already in this chapter, it rarely appears as a strategy in discussions on learning transfer. Action learning as a technique arose out of some original work by Revans (1982). Since then, other schools of practice, based on philosophies of experiential learning and critical reflection, have adapted its principles and action learning today is often loosely used as an overall term for some form of 'learning by doing'. Although a single, generally accepted definition of action learning is hard to find, it is generally described in broadly similar terms to those of Revans – as learning from concrete experience of real world problems, critically reflecting on that experience through group discussion, trial and error, discovery, and learning from and with each other. Action learning will be discussed further in Chapter 2.

## Learning in the Workplace

There is no doubt therefore that research on learning has focused greater attention than before on the study of learning in the workplace. This research, by its nature, helps examine the links between individual and organizational knowledge. It is particularly important in the context of an increasing emphasis on the development of 'knowledge workers' within organizations, and indeed the creation and maintenance of 'learning organizations'. Knowledge is now seen as a key resource, which must be generated, captured and generalized throughout the organization for effective performance. Thus the two related constructs of knowledge management and the learning organization have links with learning transfer and so will be discussed briefly here.

## KNOWLEDGE MANAGEMENT

In the same way as transferring learning from classroom to workplace requires specific, focused effort, so does transferring individual learning to organizational learning. An important part of that process is making the tacit knowledge residing in the heads of its members explicit, or, as others put it, codified. Knowledge management is therefore the process by which the knowledge, skills and expertise of people in the organization is brought to the surface and put into a form where it can be more widely distributed, and therefore available to organizational decision makers (Pan and Scarbrough 1999). It is really about the coordination of learning in different parts of the organization and its integration into organizational knowledge in order to build strategic capability.

The job of coordinating and integrating learning throughout organizations presents quite a challenge for their management. On the one hand, managers have a responsibility to drive change in order to ensure that the organization remains competitive within its business environment. On the other hand, they have a responsibility to maintain some degree of stability to ensure that cohesive strategies can be put in place and implemented. In terms of learning and knowledge transfer, this means they have to find the right balance between exploring new opportunities, which will require the creation of new knowledge, and exploiting current ones, which necessitates making explicit and widespread what the organization collectively knows already. Successful knowledge organizations are the ones that can find that balance (McKenzie and Van Winkelen 2004).

Of course 'knowledge organizations' employ 'knowledge workers', a term coined by Peter Drucker back in the 1950s. Knowledge workers are individuals with high levels of education and specialist skills combined with the ability to apply these skills to identify and solve problems. So the challenge for organizations today is not only to meet their continuing learning needs, but to ensure that these knowledge workers are prepared to use their knowledge for the benefit of the organization – in other words to maintain their levels of organizational commitment. Whilst there are undoubtedly some shining examples of organizations that can do this, unfortunately many others, and the way in which they manage their people in a controlling, hierarchical way, make the generating of organizational commitment more difficult for themselves, and in doing so inhibit the promotion of knowledge transfer.

## THE LEARNING ORGANIZATION

As already suggested, much of the knowledge or expertise organizations possess is within the heads of their people. It resides there as 'chunks' of information built up over time, and is activated by stimuli such as organizational problems that need to be solved. For the organization to transfer this knowledge into 'organizational memory' and respond to problems in a similar way, systems need to be put in place to facilitate the process.

Although not the first to describe it, Senge (1990) has certainly popularized the notion of the learning organization. He describes it as a place where people are continually expanding their capacity to achieve results, and where new thinking is constantly being encouraged and nurtured. Garvin (1993) more simply suggests it's about creating, acquiring and transferring knowledge and modifying behaviour to reflect this. The latter description has more in common with the direction of this book, dealing as it does with how conditions can be optimized to enable knowledge transfer to take place. According to Garvin, learning organizations achieve this status by the systematic solving of problems, by experimenting with new approaches, by learning from their own and others' experience, and by transferring knowledge quickly and efficiently throughout the organization.

## Creating the Commitment

Consideration of the above brings us to a really crucial point regarding learning transfer. Above all, organizations need to create the conditions where their employees can give of their best. One way in which they do this is by providing the tools and technologies that enable individuals to perform their tasks with a minimum of inconvenience. More importantly, however, are the conditions they create in terms of best leadership practices, putting the main responsibility for generating commitment firmly on the shoulders of leaders at all levels. Work on what is often called the human resources climate by, amongst others, Schneider (Schneider et al. 2003; Schneider et al. 2005) strongly indicates that the use of best practices in human resource management (setting clear and challenging goals, managing performance effectively, recognizing and rewarding effort and energizing the team to meet its challenges) as demonstrated by those leaders, facilitates knowledge sharing. These practices are instrumental in generating employee satisfaction, which in turn translates 'across the counter' to customer satisfaction and customer loyalty and thus play an important role in achieving sustainable competitive advantage.

## Frameworks for Understanding Transfer

Research undertaken in a variety of settings has identified a large number of factors that affect the transfer of learning back to the workplace. A review by Baldwin and Ford (1988), still cited extensively, is a good starting point. They based their review around three separate but related sets of factors.

### TRAINEE FACTORS

As the label suggests, these are personal characteristics of the learners that have been demonstrated to have an effect on learning transfer. They include such characteristics as self-efficacy (confidence, essentially), motivational characteristics, job and career attitudes, personality and learning styles. They will be discussed in detail in Chapter 5.

### TRAINING PROGRAMME FACTORS

These are factors that relate to the content and delivery of the learning intervention itself. Issues of interest here include the teaching of general principles, the variety of learning methods, conditions of practice and the development of adaptive expertise. Under this heading, we will also look at post-training strategies such as goal setting, self-management and coaching. These are all dealt with in Chapters 2 and 3.

### WORK ENVIRONMENT FACTORS

This category comprises such factors as support and coaching from peers and managers, organizational support for learning, and the generation and maintenance of a climate for learning transfer. We'll see more about them in Chapter 4.

Within Baldwin and Ford's framework, learning transfer (the generalization of skills and knowledge learned to the job and maintenance of those skills and knowledge over time) is affected both directly and indirectly by the above inputs. They would suggest that primarily, generalization and maintenance are dependent upon learning and retention of the training material, but that they can also be affected directly by trainee characteristics and work environment factors.

Since then, a number of models have been proposed to explain the nature of learning transfer. They will not be discussed in detail here, but instead their strengths and weaknesses will be summarized. The contribution of Broad and

Newstrom (1992) was a 3 × 3 matrix focusing on the roles of the trainer, the trainee and the trainee's manager before, during and after training. Another, from Kozlowski and Salas (1997) proposes transfer effects at three levels – individual, team or unit and organizational. They agree that complex processes are involved at each level, and that outcomes at one level combine to emerge as higher-level outcomes. A somewhat more comprehensive model, from Thayer and Teachout (1995), also deals with effects at different levels, and provides more specificity in terms of the variables seen to affect learning transfer. A meta-analytic study by Colquitt, LePine and Noe (2000) produced a model that takes account of interactions amongst learning transfer factors and their effect on transfer. Finally, a model from Holton (1996) hypothesizes that human resource development (HRD) outcomes are primarily a function of ability, motivation and environmental influences at three outcomes levels – learning, individual performance and organizational performance. The characteristics, strengths and weaknesses of these models are shown in Table 1.1.

In the course of constructing the model of learning transfer presented throughout this book, the characteristics of a number of the models outlined were considered. It is hoped that the constructed model overcomes some of the shortcomings of the others, given that it (a) is derived from practical research; (b) focuses on the most relevant factors – those that continue to turn up in the literature; and (c) concentrates on factors that can be changed, in order to make it practical and workable.

## The Learning Transfer Model

First of all, the model is presented in Figure 1.1. As with Baldwin and Ford's framework it consists of factors relating to the individual (the trainee), the training programme or intervention itself, and also to work environment factors. These factors and the relationships between them will be discussed in the chapters that follow.

To begin with, the design of the intervention, demonstrating in a practical way how the training can be best used on-the-job, combines with valid and relevant content (*programme content and design*). Offered to a participant who is ready, in the sense that they see the programme as an opportunity to learn and develop (*motivation to learn*), their *motivation to transfer*, in other words, desire to apply learning, is activated. Meanwhile in the work environment, a number of other factors exert effects. The amount of *manager support and coaching* and *peer*

**Table 1.1     Models of learning transfer**

| Model | Core Characteristics | Strengths | Weaknesses |
|---|---|---|---|
| Baldwin and Ford (1988) | Overview of transfer process | Simplicity | Generality No indication of interactions |
| Broad and Newstrom (1992) | Identifies contribution to transfer of trainee, trainer and manager | Practical focus | Explains little or nothing of the transfer process |
| Kozlowski and Salas (1997) | Indicates transfer effects at individual, team and organizational level | Recognizes complexity of transfer process and relationships between levels | Lacks specificity regarding transfer factors |
| Thayer and Teachout (1995) | Includes a range of factors discussed in the literature | Identifies factors at organizational level that influence outcomes at individual level | No indication of relative strength of factors or interactions between them |
| Colquitt, LePine and Noe (2000) | A meta-analytic study of (mainly) trainee factors | Identifies interactions amongst transfer factors Comprehensive coverage of trainee factors | Doesn't include training design factors |
| Holton (1996) | Proposes that behaviour in training is a function of ability, motivation and work environment factors | Identifies a wide range of factors and relationships amongst them Considers secondary influences on transfer | Is complex for practical use |

*support* they receive (before, during and after the programme) independently and positively affects their *motivation to transfer*. In addition, the *manager support and coaching* received facilitates them in making the time and mental space to transfer learning (*personal ability to transfer*). On top of that, the *organizational climate for transfer* will affect their desire to transfer, as well as their ability to do so. Finally, the model includes mention of *learning transfer and behaviour change* outcomes. Although learning transfer suggests change in behaviour as a primary outcome, we will see that other types of learning outcome, no less important, may also be appropriate.

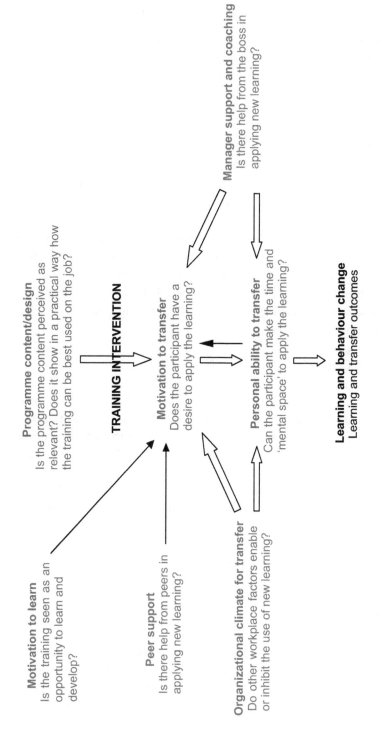

**Figure 1.1    Model of learning transfer from a training/development programme**

As we'll also see later, the model reinforces the central role of *motivation to transfer* and *personal ability to transfer* in enabling transfer to take place. Many of the factors discussed independently affect the former, which in turn directly affects the latter. These effects have been discussed separately in the literature but perhaps their collective importance has been underestimated. All of these factors will be discussed in greater detail in the following chapters. Meanwhile they are briefly described below.

## MOTIVATION TO LEARN

This factor describes the degree to which individuals are prepared to join and take part in a training or development programme. It is a personal characteristic, and is concerned primarily with perceptions they have before the programme, such as how it might relate to their needs, or what choice they have in attending it. The creation of *motivation to learn* is important for learning transfer as it has direct effects on subsequent motivation to transfer. While motivation to learn is primarily a personal characteristic, it can also be influenced indirectly by factors relating to the learning intervention itself or by work environment factors.

## PROGRAMME CONTENT AND DESIGN

This factor deals with the degree to which the programme has been designed and delivered to make it easier for participants to transfer learning back to the job. It also looks at the extent to which participants regard the programme content as appropriate to their needs. Issues such as the relevance of the content, how it builds on what the participant already knows, the credibility of the trainers or facilitators, and the balance of theory and practice are all important indicators of the likelihood of learning transfer taking place. The importance for learning transfer of appropriate content and delivery lies in matching the content to the learning needs expressed and the delivery to the various relevant characteristics of the learner and the environment in which the learning will be applied.

## MOTIVATION TO TRANSFER

This factor is about the commitment of the participant to applying back at work the skills and knowledge learned. It is affected by such questions as whether they want to apply new learning, whether they believe they can do so and whether they feel their effort will be noticed. A central factor in the model, *motivation to transfer* is perhaps influenced by more personal, programme design and work environment factors than any other. In its turn it has a strong relationship with actual learning transfer. Unless *motivation to transfer* is activated, then the chances of significant learning transfer taking place are greatly diminished.

## PERSONAL ABILITY TO TRANSFER

This factor is also central to the model, and relates to how much time, energy and mental space participants can find in their work lives to help transfer learning to the job. Although principally a personal characteristic, it can be affected by a number of other factors, particularly in the work environment. For instance, the amount of time learners get to reflect on what they learned, the amount of opportunity they get to apply that learning back at work and the amount of autonomy they have to say 'no' to distractions that prevent them from doing so will all influence the degree to which they can translate their desire (*motivation to transfer*) into reality (*personal ability to transfer*).

## MANAGER SUPPORT AND COACHING

Within the work environment, the role of the participant's manager is one that can have a significant impact on the degree to which learning transfer will be facilitated. Through feedback, support, challenge and coaching, managers of learners help to create the time and mental space so necessary for effective transfer to take place. *Manager support and coaching* plays a particularly important part immediately before and immediately after a learning event. Before the event, discussion of specific learning needs and potential applications of the learning should be on the agenda. Following the event, support for implementation of the participant's action plan and coaching to ensure the learning is consolidated are critical elements in the learning transfer process.

## PEER SUPPORT

Peers at work can also have an influence on how easy or otherwise it will be for the learner to transfer learning. *Peer support* concerns issues such as whether peers are open to new ideas, whether they provide practical support (such as filling in for their colleague while they are away on a training programme, for example) or whether they offer different perspectives that encourage experimentation and new learning. The effect of *peer support* is exerted mostly through its effect on *motivation to transfer*, and depends to a large extent on the degree of interdependency amongst the peers themselves.

## ORGANIZATIONAL CLIMATE FOR TRANSFER

This factor deals with conditions in the work environment that make it more or less conducive to the use of learning on-the-job. Components of this factor include whether the organization in general supports learning, whether particular human or financial resource constraints exist within the organization and, in general, how easy or otherwise it is to get new things implemented in the workplace. Not surprisingly, the level of support from peers and the manager will also contribute to such a climate. In turn, a positive *organizational climate for transfer* has effects on both *motivation to transfer* and *personal ability to transfer.* When such conditions exist, motivation is increased through a general level of confidence on the part of the learner that barriers to application will be surmountable, while at the same time, both the time and the mental space necessary to do so are more easily found.

## LEARNING

It's not at all uncommon that learning on a programme doesn't actually translate into changed behaviour back at work – in fact if it did all the time there would be no need for this book! However, there are times when more than one learning outcome is valid. Admittedly, for most learning interventions, the objective is a change in behaviour of some description, particularly where the development of knowledge and skills is concerned. But interventions are increasingly dealing with issues where this is not the most important outcome. For instance, at an individual level, a primary objective may be to help participants clarify their role or gain new insights into themselves. Or it may be to get them to think about their role in a completely different way. In the case of teams, to take another example, it may be important to focus on understanding personality differences between members. While behaviour change in some form may be the desired outcome ultimately, it may not be a specific outcome for the intervention. Understanding and allowing for these outcomes helps better understand the process of learning transfer.

## Summary

We began the chapter by defining learning transfer and looking at the different types of transfer that may occur following learning and development interventions. Learning transfer can be near or far, lateral or vertical, literal or figural, each with implications for the design of those interventions if successful transfer is to be achieved. We also noted the growing popularity of experiential learning, particularly in the form of constructivist learning and action learning, both of which make considerable use of the learner's prior knowledge and experience, and thus provide a more direct route to application of learning in the workplace. At an organizational level, two other developing themes have implications for learning transfer. The importance of creating conditions for knowledge to be better managed throughout the organization is one. The other, the ultimate development of a learning organization, is the hoped-for consequence. Finally, some models for learning transfer were presented, including the one that will be used as a basis for discussion of the effects of and interactions between the variety of factors that are known to affect learning transfer. These will be dealt with in the following chapters.

## References

Baldwin, T.T. and Ford, J.K. (1988). Transfer of training: A review and directions for future research. *Personnel Psychology*, 41, 63–105.

Broad, M.L. and Newstrom, J. (1992). *Transfer of training: Action-packed strategies to ensure high payoff from training investments.* New York: Addison Wesley.

Colquitt, J.A., LePine, J.R. and Noe, R.A. (2000). Trainee attributes and attitudes revisited: A meta-analysis of research on training motivation. *Journal of Applied Psychology*, 85(5), 678–707.

Garvin, D.A. (1993). Building a learning organization. *Harvard Business Review, July–August*, 78–91.

Haskell, R.E. (1998). *Reengineering corporate training: Intellectual capital and transfer of learning.* Westport, CT: Quorum Books.

Heisler, W.J. and Benham, P.O. (1992). The challenge of management development in North America in the 1990s. *Journal of Management Development*, 11, 16–31.

Holton, E.F. III. (1996). The flawed four level evaluation model. *Human Resource Development Quarterly*, 7, 5–21.

Kolb, D. (1984). *Experiential learning.* Englewood Cliffs, NJ: Prentice-Hall.

Kozlowski, S.W.J. and Salas, E. (1997). An organizational systems approach for the implementation and transfer of training. In K. Kraiger (ed.), *Creating, implementing, and managing effective training and development: State-of-the-art lessons for practice.* San Francisco: Jossey-Bass.

Marton, F. and Saljo, R. (1976). *The experience of learning. 2nd ed.* Edinburgh: Scottish Academic Press.

McKenzie, J. and Van Winkelen, C. (2004). *Understanding the knowledgeable organization: Nurturing knowledge competence.* London: Thomson.

Pan, S.L. and Scarbrough, H. (1999). Knowledge management in practice: An exploratory case study. *Technology Analysis and Strategic Management*, 11(3), 359–74.

Quinones, M.A. and Ehrenstein, A. (eds.), (1996). *Training for a rapidly changing workplace: Applications of psychological research.* Washington, DC: American Psychological Association.

Revans, R.W. (1982). *The origins and growth of action learning.* London: Chartwell-Bratt.

Schneider, B., Godfrey, M.G., Hayes, S.C., Huang, M., Lim, B., Nishii, L.H., Raver, J.L. and Ziegert, J.C. (2003). The human side of strategy: Employee experiences of strategic alignment in a service organization. *Journal of Applied Psychology*, 88(5), 836–50.

Schneider, B., Ehrhart, M.G., Mayer, D.M., Saltz, J.L. and Niles-Jolly, K. (2005). Understanding organization-customer links in service settings. *Academy of Management Journal*, 48(6), 1017–32.

Senge, P.M. (1990). *The fifth discipline: The art and practice of the learning organization.* New York: Doubleday.

Thayer, P.W. and Teachout, M.S. (1995). A climate for transfer model. (AL/IIR-TP-1995-0035). Brooks Air Force Base, TX. Technical Training Research Division, Armstrong Laboratory. In K. Kraiger (ed.), *Creating, implementing, and managing effective training and development: State-of-the-art lessons for practice.* San Francisco: Jossey-Bass.

# 2

# Getting the Programme Right

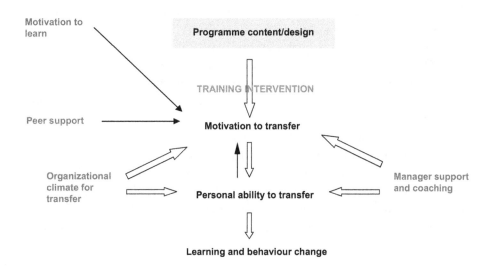

Motivation to learn

**Programme content/design**

TRAINING INTERVENTION

Peer support

**Motivation to transfer**

Organizational climate for transfer

**Personal ability to transfer**

Manager support and coaching

Learning and behaviour change

## Introduction

It is probably fair to say that much of the emphasis on training programmes today is on the content and delivery of those programmes – what actually happens in the classroom. The bookstores, libraries and databases full of books, articles and 'how to' manuals of every description that concentrate on the various tools and techniques for delivering training are clear evidence of this emphasis. Of course, no one would argue that a properly thought-out and well-delivered programme is a key contributor to its success, whatever the influence of other factors on learning transfer. If an appropriate analysis of the skills and knowledge needed has been conducted, the content of the programme will reflect those needs, and will constitute a major element in meeting them. If in addition the design of the programme has been based on principles that optimize the chances for learning transfer, then a significant amount of the work will have been achieved by the end of the programme. So, the focus in this chapter will be on the principles of learning design and delivery that have the most relevance for the attainment of learning transfer. Understanding these principles should provide a sound basis for choosing the appropriate content, tools and techniques that have been proven to work, rather than leaving participants at the mercy of the trainer's preferences!

## Programme Content

Without a doubt, a proper assessment of training needs should take place in the first instance. Training Needs Analyses (TNAs) can vary greatly in their degree of complexity and sophistication, and can be approached in many ways. Ultimately, however, their purpose is the same – to ensure as close a match as possible between what is delivered on the day and what those attending actually need. Although the complexity varies, a decent training needs analysis will be conducted from a number of viewpoints, in order to increase the probability that information being gathered is accurate and reliable. At the heart of the more sophisticated TNAs, one of many forms of job analysis, for example functional job analysis or critical incidents methodology is often used. Job analysis can help identify the human behaviours necessary for adequate and for superior job performance. From these, the types of skills, knowledge and other attributes necessary to perform the job can be determined.

However, it is not always feasible or indeed practical to undertake a comprehensive job analysis as part of training needs identification. If the organization is small, or the type of training being considered is not on such a grand scale, then a more simple analysis might be undertaken. At the very least, though, it should include the following:

### INTERVIEWS WITH KEY PEOPLE

At the outset, the views of those such as the CEO, divisional managers, senior human resources professionals, and so on should be sought. The purpose of meeting with these people would be to get a clear picture of the organization's strategic direction and its implications for training, development and staff mobility. The meetings could also consider their view of the appropriate knowledge and skills available in the organization at present, and any other indicators (internal or external) of training and development needs.

## STAFF GROUP MEETINGS

As a follow up to the meetings with key senior people, meetings with other staff, usually in groups (otherwise the process becomes very time-consuming, and doesn't necessarily result in better data) can be very useful. Best results are usually achieved if the groups are organized in terms of similar needs, such as management, frontline staff or shop-floor operatives, thus enabling a more specific focus for the meetings. Facilitated groups comprising 8–12 staff, using a structured questioning process over a period of perhaps 2 hours can generate a lot of valuable information regarding training and development needs for current and future roles, and the ways in which these needs might be met.

## NEEDS ANALYSIS QUESTIONNAIRE

An additional option, particularly to include those not taking part in the needs identification group sessions, but who wish to have an input, would be to use a relatively simple questionnaire which they could complete. It need contain no more than five or six questions about what training and development needs they have and how they feel those needs might be met.

## Objectives and Outcomes

Assuming you have undertaken some form of needs analysis, the next important step is to set clear objectives for the training you propose to deliver. Transfer is more likely to occur if objectives are 'application-oriented' – stated in terms of what participants should be able to do on return to their jobs (assuming the opportunities to do so are provided). This should happen with individual content areas as well as the overall programme. In addition to facilitating transfer, it also makes measurement of that transfer easier. For example, a training needs analysis might indicate that managers in a particular department need to 'communicate better with their staff'. That's all very well, but what does it look like in practice? Is it about what they say or don't say in meetings? Is it about the frequency of communication? Is it about style? Training designers, by forcing themselves to think in specific terms what 'communicating better' looks like in practice, can then design a more appropriate intervention to meet the need. The process will almost certainly involve asking more questions about the need, which in turn will strengthen the response to that need. Lastly, the designers may wish to run a pilot programme, either in part or in full. This can serve in effect as an extension of the needs analysis process, and enables both

## BOX 2.1: THE VALUE OF PROPER TRAINING NEEDS ANALYSIS

An evaluation of the training and development activity for the previous year was recently undertaken for a local authority employing some 400 people. The data gathered from meetings with senior managers and groups of staff at all levels clearly pointed to a lack of integration between the training opportunities provided (which were not inconsiderable) and the individual and organizational needs behind them. What the evaluation showed was that:

- Staff members in the authority generally took the initiative themselves with regard to what courses, programmes or conferences they wanted to attend (all training and development activity is conducted by external providers).
- In theory, the approval process meant that their interest in attending should be discussed with their line manager, who would decide whether or not attendance was appropriate. In reality, however, the vast majority of line managers never really became involved in the process, giving approval to attend in most cases as long as the budget allowed for it.
- As a result, when staff members returned from the programme or conference, there was little or (more likely) no follow-up, with the resultant loss of learning to the authority as a whole.
- An overall training and development needs analysis conducted as part of the evaluation demonstrated that the range of interventions attended by staff of the authority was not reflected in the range of individual and organizational needs identified through interviews and focus groups, with consequent waste of financial resources.

Recommendations following the analysis included the creation of a clear process for ensuring that the people who attend training courses and other learning events are the right people in the right place at the right time. This was to ensure better integration between the needs of the organization, the (real) training and development needs of the individual, and the training attended; a greater chance of the training content being perceived as appropriate, and the training delivery better geared to the needs of particular participants; and better application and maintenance of learning from the training.

A follow-up review a year later showed that important progress had been made in this regard. A meeting template had been designed to assist line managers, providing them with a set of questions to be asked of the intending participant at a pre-course meeting, intended to assess the need in greater detail. The meeting is now used to identify reasons for attending the chosen learning event, the main areas for development, participant expectations and possible applications of learning and how the event might be used to address these. Within the HR department, the applications are now also screened to determine whether they are in line with stated organizational training and development needs. All in all, the process is a much tighter one than before, enabling greater concentration of training resources on areas of greatest importance.

the designer of the programme and the client of the programme to see if the reality measures up to the concept. Pilot programmes can be very valuable, and evaluation of pilot programmes can identify the most relevant content areas and make suggestions for future programmes.

Having said that, it is not always possible to be clear what particular learning outcomes should look like in practice. For example, with programmes that are concerned with more complex knowledge and skills, such as management development programmes, more than one type of learning outcome might be appropriate, and may be hard to measure. To take some particular instances, in the course of reviewing a number of leadership development programmes in recent years, this author has encountered learning outcomes such as a total reassessment of his competence in a particular area for one person, a significant redefinition of her management role in the case of another, and in a third case a decision on a complete change of career path.

## A Question of Balance

One important balance to be struck when deciding on the content of training and development programmes is that between the theoretical and the practical. For example, participants on a coaching workshop may want to know how to give performance feedback effectively. There are steps to be followed, words to be used and avoided, and a time and place for it to happen. Repeated practice of these steps will certainly help. This type of knowledge is known as *procedural knowledge,* or knowledge of *how* to do it. However, this type of knowledge is only good up to a point. In reality, if the situations that the participant encounters do not reflect exactly the conditions of the situations in training, they may not know what to do. This is where the teaching of another type of knowledge, *declarative knowledge,* is important. Acquiring declarative knowledge refers to learning the underlying principles of a particular skill, such as the importance of feedback, its role in the maintenance of self-efficacy and motivation, and so on. Research has clearly demonstrated (Smith and Ragan 1993; Schunk 1996) that transfer is more effective when there is exposure to both types of knowledge in training. This works in two ways. By introducing the general principles relating to a particular skill (salary negotiating, for example) learners can link those general principles to what they already know in other areas, such as sales negotiating. They will also recognize what's different about the two. Understanding the principles will also make it easier for them to see *why* different steps are followed, and to discover why a certain course of action might not be working.

In practice, many well-delivered training and development programmes get the balance right. What is not uncommon to hear either is that after a programme, participants report that although they may not have learned anything new (in their view), they feel they now have a framework (the declarative knowledge) into which to place their (procedural) knowledge and skills. Having this framework gives them confidence that what they were already doing was in fact good practice. So for a participant, the topic may not be new, but either the declarative or procedural aspect of it might be.

This is related to the question of how much theory should be included in training and development programmes. Evidence suggests that the proper balance (unless the aim of the programme is to provide theoretical knowledge) seems to be to provide just enough to enable understanding of the practice. This fulfils the need for sufficient declarative knowledge to understand principles and models, while at the same time the learner doesn't get lost in a sea of theory.

## Programme Design

The other important issue for the classroom relates to how the programme is actually run. Effective programme designs will be those that make it easier for participants to use the learning in a practical way back at work. As mentioned in the introduction, application of specific skills in specific contexts, such as using a spreadsheet in an accountant's office, or making a hotel booking in a travel agency, is not usually subject to the same challenges as is the application of more complex knowledge and skills of the type found on management development-type programmes. Therefore, the focus in this section will be more on designs that facilitate transfer of the latter.

### IDENTICAL ELEMENTS

It's as far back as the beginning of the last century that Thorndike and Woodworth (1901) indicated that the presence of 'identical elements' in the training and transfer settings helps retain both motor and verbal skills. In other words, learning transfer will be greater the more similar the training situation and the reality (Gick and Holyoak 1987; Butterfield and Nelson 1989). Airline pilot training demonstrates this principle very clearly. As airlines cannot take a chance on trainees causing death and destruction as they learn, very sophisticated systems (simulators, for example) are put in place to make the training situation as close as possible to the reality. In the same vein, but closer to the ground, many organizations now use professional actors for skills development in conflict handling and performance management. Of course, with management skills, many training situations take place away from the workplace, and indeed many training methods, such as outdoor development or management games, are at quite a distance. How transfer is dealt with in these cases will be discussed later.

## PRACTISE, PRACTISE, PRACTISE

Another response to the problem of applying complex skills can be dealt with by breaking those skills down to their simpler components and practising their application. Overlearning is about providing trainees with continued practice far beyond the point where the task has been performed successfully. The greater the amount of overlearning, the greater will be the retention of the training material. Different studies (Myers and Fisk 1987; Proctor and Dutta 1995) have shown that extensive practice on learning components that are consistent across different situations allows skill 'automaticity' (Anderson 1995) to develop, and thus allows more attention and memory to be focused on the inconsistent elements of the tasks to be performed. This automaticity is really the third stage (the development of declarative and procedural knowledge being the first two) in effective skill application. In sports settings, for example, we see even the best golfers, tennis players and other athletes continually practise their swings and strokes – what they are doing is keeping up that level of automaticity so that they'll still be able to do it when the pressure comes on.

One implication this has for management-type training relates to the amount of time for practice of new skills (some of them quite complex) in most training courses. Unless the workshop is dedicated to development of that skill, it is often the case that trainers only allow enough time for the trainee to become broadly familiar with the principles (declarative knowledge), encouraging them to 'have a go' at the skill (procedural knowledge), but not devoting sufficient time to its practice for the trainee to become really competent (automaticity). Once again, if the objectives of the workshop are stated in behavioural terms, everyone will be clearer on what is the intended learning outcome.

## KEEP 'EM INTERESTED

Of course, practising the same skill over and over again can be hard going, even for the most dedicated, so different ways of approaching learning need to be considered in any programme. From a long time back (Duncan 1958; Shore and Sechrest 1961) the research has told us that learning is more easily transferred to the workplace when a variety of relevant training methods are used. This can manifest itself in different ways. For example, using several different examples of a concept to be learned improves trainees' understanding to the extent that they will be more able to see the applicability of a concept in a new situation. More recently, cognitive approaches have added the understanding that high variability of examples, while it may hinder initial learning, will actually enhance transfer (Elio and Anderson 1984; Schmidt and Bjork 1992). Interestingly, conditions that provide added difficulty for learners, such as varying the training method, tend to result in poor immediate performance but better performance in the longer term. Conversely, consistently using the same method of training throughout a programme will result in better immediate performance but poorer long-term performance. The same applies to training methods that show the 'right' and the 'wrong' ways of applying a skill. Trainees shown (and indeed practising) both the 'right' and 'wrong' ways will be likely to apply it significantly better at work (Baldwin 1992) than those who are only shown the 'right' way.

The implications of this knowledge for learning transfer are clear enough. It's probably true to say that most trainers deliver their training programmes using a variety of different methods to facilitate learning. This is very important as what the research also shows is that in a general sense, the *variety* of methods used is indeed more important than the *actual* methods used. A study undertaken in a major US organization (Bretz and Thompsett 1992) around a programme that used an integrative learning approach (sometimes called accelerated learning or super learning) bears this out. The researchers provided a relaxed, informal atmosphere, and the programme was delivered in an atmosphere of 'fun'. This was compared with a more traditional environment of lecture and questions. Although participants reacted more favourably to the integrative learning approach, both groups performed significantly better than a no-treatment control group, and no differences between approaches in terms of learning transfer were observed.

## USING ANALOGIES

One consistent element of training delivery over the years is the use of games, simulations and other exercises as vehicles for learning. While one valid reason for using these methods is to enable variety, another may be the value they have as analogies for learning points. For example, it's quite common to look at modern organizations as 'organisms', influencing and in turn being influenced by their environment. A common analogy when discussing organizational change is to describe the organization as an 'iceberg' in order to demonstrate its more deeply-rooted (and therefore harder to change) aspects. Indeed our much-maligned management jargon speaks of the coal face (the front line, which is itself surely an analogy), blue-skies thinking (generating creative ideas, presumably unencumbered by clouds) and many more.

However, dealing in analogies (in moderation) can be helpful for learning transfer, and the evidence that's around (Thompson, Gentner and Lowenstein 2000; Nadler, Thompson and Van Boven 2003) appears to support this. Their studies found that presenting different problem cases with similar principles involved in their solution in negotiating skills training resulted in a greater level of learning transfer than giving straightforward advice on how to conduct negotiations. In fact they found that subjects experiencing the former strategy were nearly three times more likely to transfer, as measured in post-training role-plays. It's probable that some of the transfer effect of using analogies comes not just from the novelty of using a different method, but also from the introduction of general principles (declarative knowledge) discussed earlier.

## DISTRIBUTED VERSUS MASSED LEARNING

This distinction concerns whether it's better for learning events to be divided into separate segments or modules, or instead delivered all in one go. For example, a supervisory training course could be 'distributed', that is, conducted say for one day a week for 12 weeks, or 'massed', meaning that it's conducted all together over 2 weeks. Research over the years (Jacoby 1978; Naylor and Briggs 1983; Enos, Kehrhahn and Bell 2003) seems to confirm that, for more effective transfer, learning acquired under 'distributed' conditions lasts longer than learning acquired under 'massed' conditions.

This shouldn't be too surprising. Programmes that allow, say, a few weeks between modules give participants time to advance work-related projects, or to try out something they've learned, such as chairing a meeting or giving feedback to a staff member. Participants can then be in a position to report back to their fellow learners at the next module, and use them for guidance and support.

## GOOD FACILITATION

It goes without saying that not everyone can be an effective facilitator, despite some people's opinions regarding their own level of ability. It has been demonstrated time and time again that with adult learners, so-called 'adult learning' approaches offer the best (indeed probably the only) chance of learners maintaining what they learn back on-the-job. Adult learning approaches involve a number of elements (MacDonald, Gabriel and Cousins 2000), the more important ones being:

- Recognition and use of the learners' experience

- Ensuring learning programme flexibility

- Conducting effective group discussions

- Ensuring relevant and applicable content

- Using a modular structure.

Given what we've seen already about what helps learning transfer, this is to be expected. Adult learning approaches require those conducting the learning intervention to act more as a support for the learner than the 'expert' with all the knowledge. In most adult learning situations, the learners have a wealth of varied experience to draw on, into which they can place new learning

---

**BOX 2.2: GETTING THE MOST FROM PEERS**

A feature of almost all leadership development programmes conducted by this author over the last 10 years has been the value participants repeatedly state they gain from meeting others from a variety of backgrounds, but facing similar issues. This has been true for programmes delivered within many different types of organization, ranging from a small financial services organization to a large international public service body. A number of conditions seem to be common in all these cases. To begin with, all of the programmes have been delivered on a distributed basis, that is, over a period of several weeks or months, involving a number of meetings with time back at work in between. Feedback from participants suggests that this type of programme structure greatly facilitates the process, particularly the fact that participants have time to develop collegial relationships with other participants. During the days they meet up, they have the opportunity to discuss their respective work environments, the issues they face, and will often be offered advice from other participants on how to address them. Feedback also indicates that this benefit can be further enhanced if the programme is residential. Finally, even on programmes not formally adopting an action learning methodology, the use of participant-led cases as a basis for mutual learning has been considered a critical element in aiding learning transfer.

experiences. To take an example, a facilitator using adult learning methods may be trying to help learners understand why empirically derived evidence concerning some aspect of management (such as human motivation) explains and predicts what will happen in a given situation, rather than the learners' own intuitive knowledge. In attempting to do so, the facilitator will have a greater chance of success by first understanding what the learners already know, and engaging in dialogue to build on that. The process of dialogue is very important in enabling the learner to acquire the necessary knowledge, and understanding evolves through questioning and explanation, through challenging (by both learner and facilitator), and through support and feedback. Training designs that promote this type of learning will challenge learners to be more active, to interact with their peers, and to continually search for meaning – all very helpful for transfer.

Facilitators who are credible are also able to demonstrate significant knowledge of the world in which their learners work. This works together with a facilitative style ('facilitation of learning' rather than 'teaching') to make a positive impact. Skilled facilitators draw a lot on course participants' current knowledge and experience as a basis for learning. They also draw a balance between bringing issues to the surface so that they can be discussed openly, and setting ground rules that ensure confidentiality is maintained within the group. This helps to generate trust in the facilitators' capability, which in turn helps participants' satisfaction with the learning process.

## ACTION LEARNING

One approach to learning in which adult learning principles play a significant role is that of action learning (the essence of which was outlined in Chapter 1). Smith and O'Neil (2003a; 2003b), for example, in a useful summary of the nature of action learning programmes, describe them in terms of the following characteristics:

- Participants tackle real problems

- Participants meet in small stable learning groups

- Each set holds intermittent meetings over a fixed programme cycle

- Problems are relevant to a participant's own workplace realities

- A supportive collaborative learning process is followed in a set

- The process is based on reflection, questioning, and refutation

- Participants take action between set meetings to resolve their problem.

A focus on personal learning outcomes is also an important characteristic of action learning interventions (Pedler 1997). He argues that action learning outcomes should be stated in developmental terms, and should consider the learning or changes that take place both within and as a result of the intervention. He also feels that evaluation of such interventions should be conducted by the participants in the exercise, in order to help them become more aware of their own learning. While action learning interventions may sometimes receive less favourable ratings from participants (they do after all require hard work) on some dimensions (Jennings 2002), their real world learning credentials are in no doubt. Other evaluations of action learning interventions (Wills and Oliver 1996; Yorks et al. 1998), have demonstrated various positive outcomes such as cost savings and value added from implementation of action learning projects, as well as other important personal learning outcomes. By building on participants' experience, using their expertise, and rooting the training content in real world problems, motivation to learn and motivation to transfer are thus enhanced.

The link between action learning and learning transfer lies in the philosophy of action learning, in which desired outcomes are the 'doing of something different', put succinctly by Johnson (1998, 297). 'Only when we can transfer our knowledge, skill, behaviours, beliefs, or insights to something practical, thus providing evidence that we are able to apply it, can we claim that we have really learned. In other words, learning is about changing.' Given this description, the value of action learning as a technique, particularly where complex skills and knowledge are concerned, can be seen. In these situations there is a large degree of overlap between the learning situation and the application situation, and so many of the barriers to transfer that might otherwise be in place are already dealt with.

## ADAPTIVE EXPERTISE

In Chapter 1 we looked the main differences between behavioural and cognitive approaches to learning and transfer, with the latter focusing more

---

**BOX 2.3: THE VALUE OF ACTION LEARNING**

As a design aspect of a management development programme for health service managers, delivered over a period of several months, participants were divided into action learning sets and asked to work in those sets on their own work-related problems. During the course of their meetings, they addressed a number of issues relevant to set members, which related to problems such as the management of difficult staff members, team motivation and dealing with organizational politics. Although self-facilitated (they didn't have an external set advisor, a regular feature of action learning sets) they nevertheless used a number of techniques common to action learning introduced on the programme including critical reflection, active listening and giving feedback. An evaluation of the programme, conducted some months later reported positive reactions from all sets to this approach to learning. In some of the situations reported, members said they felt extremely positive at the end of the process, as they had found solutions to issues they had raised with the set. Others were positive because the set members had reinforced their view that the course of action they (the problem holder) were taking was appropriate and were given the confidence to continue with it. Still others felt that they had been encouraged to look at the issue they brought to the set in a different way, offering different perceptions and options for solution. All of them felt that the opportunity they had to try things and then report back to the set for guidance, support or feedback was immensely helpful, making the learning journey from classroom to application much shorter.

---

on learners' mental processes rather than the similarity between training and performance conditions. The cognitive approach is particularly important in the development of what is called adaptive expertise (Holyoak 1991), which relates to the learner's ability to respond successfully to changes in the nature of the trained task. In effect, this means individuals learning *what* to do (procedural knowledge) as well as learning *why* they should do it (declarative knowledge). This involves mindful processing and abstraction. It's becoming more important in management training and development as, for instance, it has been suggested (Mainemelis, Boyatzis and Kolb 2002) that job performance is becoming increasingly dependent on managers' ability to adapt to changing conditions, technologies and contexts. Unfortunately, many training programmes use methods that are aimed at the acquisition of procedural rather than declarative knowledge. These methods, whilst facilitating near transfer, actually inhibit far transfer. The development of adaptive expertise should be particularly relevant in the context of more complex skills and knowledge that are integral to management development-type training.

Two other cognitive processes are important in the development of adaptive expertise – the development of knowledge structures, and the building of what are called metacognitive skills. With regard to knowledge structures (also called mental models or cognitive maps), for instance, experts differ from novices in terms of how their knowledge is structured in the brain. According to Kraiger, Ford and Salas (1993), as individuals gain experience at a task, their declarative knowledge becomes compiled into procedural rules and is meaningfully structured in memory. For experts, the knowledge structures built in this way contain both problem definitions and solutions; for novices, these structures tend to be separate. Thus it is easier for experts to identify when a particular strategy is appropriate or inappropriate in a given situation. In practice, this is what's happening when we turn to the colleague who 'always knows what to do in a crisis'. We probably all know what to do if given sufficient time to think through the problem and its solution. However, the expert has usually a number of mental models in which similar problems and their respective solutions are stored together. So, when quick thinking and immediate action is required, they have a solution.

Experts also appear to have better metacognitive skills than novices. Metacognition is a cognitive function that includes an awareness and understanding of the relationship between the task requirements and one's individual capabilities. It also includes a control function of planning, monitoring and regulating strategies. Thus experts are better able to recognize differences or changes, and adapt their responses to the task accordingly. Imagine, to take a simple example, a new solicitor trying to get to grips with a particular aspect of company law. Being a reflective type of learner, they choose to read as much as they can on the subject. However, as time goes on, they discover that less and less of what they read is sticking in their mind, despite reading particular sections over and over again, and that they are now beginning to get confused. The higher the level of metacognitive skill they possess, the more likely they are to realize the difficulty and change the way they learn (by also talking to an expert for example) rather than accepting it and staying with the same learning strategy. Research by Enos, Kehrhahn and Bell (2003) points to the importance of metacognition in successful learning and transfer outcomes.

## In Practice

So, how can the results of all the research undertaken and described above be put to practical use? What follows are some recommendations regarding a number of strategies that designers and facilitators of learning events should integrate into these events to increase the chances that the resulting learning will be applied back at work.

## ASSESS THE TRAINING NEED

It's critical to ensure that an adequate training needs analysis takes place before embarking on any training initiative. At the very least, this should include some conversations with relevant people or other diagnosis of the skills and knowledge gap the initiative is intended to close. While intending participants are usually the main people to consult with, their line managers and perhaps their staff (if appropriate) can also provide an important perspective. For frontline training, feedback from customers can be an excellent starting point. The more sources that can be used, the better, as this will increase the validity of the information supporting the need, and thus increase the motivation to learn.

## SET CLEAR OBJECTIVES FOR THE TRAINING YOU PROPOSE TO DELIVER

Once the content is agreed, clear, application-oriented objectives are the best way to proceed. They will enable both the provider and the trainee to be clear about how the learning on the programme is intended to be used back at work. Application-oriented objectives are those that focus on what the learner should be able to do on their return to work, rather than simply what they should know by the end of the course. They are particularly important if critical skills are required to be developed, say for example where safety or emergency procedures are involved. Application of these skills in (real) work settings may be much more difficult than their application in the classroom. Focusing on how they will be applied at work rather than in training increases the chances that sufficient time will be given to the development of the skill (including overlearning or the development of adaptive expertise if necessary) and that conditions in the training and the work setting will be as alike as possible (identical elements). Setting objectives in this way also makes training evaluation at the behavioural (on-the-job) level easier, by providing greater clarity around the conditions under which the trained task is to be performed.

## REMEMBER THAT MORE THAN ONE TYPE OF LEARNING OUTCOME MIGHT BE APPROPRIATE

As a starting point, application-oriented objectives make a lot of sense, as they provide a clearer picture of the desired outcome of the training. It's also important to bear in mind that for some interventions, objectives that are not easily measurable in behavioural terms may also be appropriate. However, that doesn't mean they should be ignored. If, for example, one hopes that attendance at a workshop for frontline staff will help promote a new attitude towards customers or that executives on a leadership programme will better understand the company's vision of the future, the more clarity that can be provided about what they might look like in practice the better.

## BALANCE THE CONTENT IN TERMS OF THEORETICAL AND PRACTICAL KNOWLEDGE

In order for participants to generalize and maintain their new learning back at work, an appropriate balance of declarative (knowing) and procedural (doing) knowledge should be struck. The balance struck will of course depend on the nature of the learning event. On a senior management programme, for instance, a session on strategy might concentrate on what's in the academic literature, with the sole purpose of stimulating thinking around the different approaches available. At the other end of the scale, a practical session on giving performance feedback may spend the entire time practising the skill, with little formal input. However, as a general guideline, enough theory just to put more practical aspects into context is usually the most effective.

## PROVIDE RELEVANT REFERENCE MATERIAL

Despite a feeling amongst trainers that a majority of participants put the paper in the recycling bin and give the folders to their kids for school, there is at least anecdotal evidence that significant numbers of participants do actually refer to some of the material they receive on programmes they have attended. Experience suggests that reference material in the form of job aids in a form that's easy to get at has the best chance of being reviewed. Examples of such aids are pocket-sized handbooks (called names like *Twenty Tips for Trainers* or *The Ten Commandments of Selling*); advice or memory joggers in the form of mnemonics or acronyms (SMART for goal setting is a favourite); or models that are easy to remember (such as the 7-S model for analyzing organizations). Photominutes (digital photographs of the contents of flipcharts used during the session) are also popular.

## ENCOURAGE PRE-COURSE WORK

It is almost always beneficial for participants to begin engaging in a programme before they actually attend it. Relevant reading is one example. As well as giving an indication of salient programme content issues, it can facilitate participants in thinking about how the content can apply in their own work situation, and enable them to form questions for later clarification. Participants can also be asked to think about certain aspects of programme content through recalling critical incidents (such as a difficult industrial relations issue) and how they were handled. This reflective activity helps highlight relevant strengths as well as areas for development. This is also usually the appropriate time to complete relevant instruments such as competency profiles (perhaps to be used for post-programme comparison), personality profiles or learning styles questionnaires.

## DELIVER THE PROGRAMME IN MODULAR FORM

On the basis that distributed training seems to be better for learning transfer than massed training, consideration should be given to delivering an intervention in modules. This of course throws up a number of logistical difficulties which must be balanced against the intervention's objectives and likely outcomes. For longer programmes, delivering modules of perhaps 2 or 3 days at a time, with a break of at least a week between modules, can facilitate learning transfer. The time between modules allows the opportunity for reflection, for practice and feedback and for consolidation of learning on-the-job. A word of warning though – if this approach is taken, it is usually better to be prescriptive about what participants should undertake between modules. Having a specific action to complete, such as chairing a meeting in a new format, and writing up the outcome as a critical incident, will focus participants on the application of their learning. Time should then be set aside at the next module for feedback, guidance and support.

## MAKE THE TRAINING AS RELEVANT TO THE WORK SITUATION AS POSSIBLE

It should go without saying, but examples, cases and incidents used in an intervention should as far as possible relate to the real-life work situation of participants. One way of ensuring this is to use cases developed by participants themselves from their own experience. When examples are used which go outside this experience (such as a 'lost at sea' or 'desert survival' exercise), clear links should be made between the learning from the example and its application to work. In using such material, the facilitators also need to be aware of the diversity of work backgrounds and situations of participants, such as whether their organizations are simple or complex, hierarchical or adaptive, and so on. Taking care of these issues will, as well as increasing the credibility of the facilitators, improve the transfer of learning.

## VARY THE TRAINING METHODS AND MEDIA

As far as is practicable, and in keeping with other recommendations, a variety of different methods and media should be used to take account of participants' different learning styles. Participants in general tend to be doers or thinkers, and so a balance of inputs that exercises both preferences will help maintain interest and facilitate learning. Appropriate guest speakers can also add variety. However, an important point to watch out for with guest speakers is that for them to contribute significantly to participants' learning both their content and presentation quality need to be high. The most knowledgeable experts will fail to impress if their communication skills don't match their expertise, while even the most polished presenters will have trouble influencing their audience if their material doesn't stand up to scrutiny.

## PROVIDE 'IDEAS AND APPLICATIONS' NOTEBOOKS

An increasingly popular option on training and development programmes is to provide the opportunity for participants to systematically note new ideas and applications as they arise during the programme. Sometimes known as keeping a reflective journal or learning log, the activity provides a small piece of 'mental space' (perhaps at the end of each distinct session) to gather one's thoughts about a topic and record them while still fresh. This will help with the retention of important learning, but just as importantly, it can serve as an input to action planning later on.

## HAVE PARTICIPANTS CREATE AN ACTION PLAN

An appropriate amount of time should be given within the programme for participants to formulate a (SMART) action plan, which should include specific actions to be taken to ensure the application of skills learned. Perhaps incorporated as part of this could be a 'relapse prevention' session to help participants identify potential barriers to application of learning and possible ways of overcoming them. The creation of action plans and the use of relapse prevention sessions will be discussed more fully in Chapter 3.

## INCLUDE SOME INTER-MODULE APPLICATION WORK

Work to be completed between modules of a multi-module programme can serve two purposes relating to learning transfer. At an organizational level, work-based projects or other assignments (group or individual) can be undertaken, which aim to apply learning from the programme to a real world problem, such as absenteeism or falling sales. In these situations, guidelines regarding the purpose and scope of the assignment should be clear and the work to be undertaken manageable in the time allowed. With more in-depth assignments, it's typical that participants have a period of months to complete them, and their presentation forms the basis of a follow-up and review module. At an individual level, the work can be in the form of specific work activity to be undertaken to develop particular competencies, called a competency development plan (CDP) or personal development plan (PDP). In this instance, learning objectives are set, the appropriate learning method(s) chosen, and the achievement of objectives and consequent learning documented and reflected upon.

## PROVIDE OPPORTUNITIES TO PRACTISE

Despite the evidence concerning the need for repeated practice so that skill automaticity will develop, it's still quite common for training programmes involved in skill development to only practise the skills enough so that the participant 'seems to be getting the hang of it'. In these instances it is less likely that the skill will survive the transition to the workplace, much less be

---

### BOX 2.4: THE CASE FOR ON-THE-JOB PROJECTS

The use of practical work-based assignments as components of learning interventions is becoming increasingly popular. A strong argument for their inclusion is both the development of critical thinking skills and the application of theory to real world practice. In learning transfer terms, the intention is often to achieve this through the development of adaptive expertise, which is about balancing the conceptual and practical aspects of one's learning style. Typically, work-based assignments involve participants choosing a real world issue in need of attention back in their workplace. This issue is put in a declarative context and relevant frameworks or theories by which the problem might be explained are applied.

An example of this could be dealing with a team motivation issue through the application of expectancy theory. In moving back and forth between the theory and the practice, the problem holder is learning more about where the theory might apply or not, is thinking about possible solutions to the problem as well as knowledge structures for understanding it, and is perhaps discovering new views of the problem they didn't already have. They may also have the opportunity to try out some of these solutions and monitor the results. The reflective process that accompanies the practical experimentation is what leads to real learning and transfer.

maintained over a period of time. If skill application is really the learning goal, then within the programme participants need sufficient opportunity to practise it, using perhaps 80 per cent of the time allotted on practice, with the other 20 per cent on background and explanation. During practice, the probability of learning transfer will also be enhanced if they 'get it wrong' as well as right, so practice scenarios should take account of this.

## CONSIDER INCLUDING AN ACTION LEARNING COMPONENT

As we have seen, action learning as a learning tool has proved to be very effective on certain types of programmes, where personal development is also a consideration. Action learning techniques are specific and require facilitators to clearly understand their principles and operation, in order for them to be able to provide clear and appropriate learning support to participants.

## Summary

In summary, we have seen that there are many things that can be done to increase the likelihood of learning being applied back at work. Firstly, programmes can include a variety of training and learning methods. These can range from the more traditional, such as presentation, discussion, and role play to the more cognitively-oriented, such as using analogies and guided discovery. Secondly, programmes that distribute their training over a period of time (particularly those that allow time for reflection and application in between sessions) will, according to the evidence, provide greater opportunity to apply learning back at work. Thirdly, where the designed programmes have a practical skill component, it is important that plenty of time is allowed for practice, ideally to a level where those skills become automatic. Using examples of 'how-not-to-do-it' as well as 'the right way' will enhance this learning. Furthermore, placing the skills learning and practice within a theoretical framework, to enable participants to grasp the underlying principles will give better results. Particularly where broader and more complex knowledge and skills are concerned, using analogical models in training will enhance learning and transfer. This is one way of getting participants to think more broadly, and to link learning in one domain to learning in another. It is the strengthening of these connections that makes the difference. The hoped-for final outcome from the use of all these techniques is to develop adaptive expertise – trainees' ability to adapt to changing conditions and contexts – a competence that is becoming more in demand as organizations develop.

## References

Anderson, J.R. (1995). *Learning and memory: An integrated approach.* New York: Alley.

Baldwin, T.T. (1992). Effects of alternative modeling strategies on outcomes of interpersonal training. *Journal of Applied Psychology, 77,* 147–54.

Bretz, R.D. and Thompsett, R.E. (1992). Comparing traditional and integrative learning methods in organizational training programs. *Journal of Applied Psychology, 77*(6), 941–51.

Butterfield, E.C. and Nelson, G.D. (1989). Theory and practice of teaching for transfer. *Educational Technology Research and Development, 37,* 5–38.

Duncan, C.P. (1958). Transfer after training with single versus multiple tasks. In T.T. Baldwin and J.K. Ford (1988), Transfer of training: A review and directions for future research. *Personnel Psychology, 41,* 63–105.

Elio, R. and Anderson, J.R. (1984). The effects of information order and learning mode on schema abstraction. In M.A. Quinones and A. Ehrenstein (eds.), *Training for a rapidly changing workplace: Applications of psychological research.* Washington, DC: American Psychological Association.

Enos, M.D., Kehrhahn, M.T. and Bell, A. (2003). Informal learning and the transfer of learning: How managers develop proficiency. *Human Resource Development Quarterly, 14*(4), 369–88.

Gick, M.L. and Holyoak, K.J. (1987). The cognitive basis of knowledge transfer. In M.A. Quinones and A. Ehrenstein (eds.), *Training for a rapidly changing workplace: Applications of psychological research.* Washington, DC: American Psychological Association.

Holyoak, K.J. (1991). Symbolic connectionism: Toward third-generation theories of expertise. In K.A. Ericsson and J. Smith (eds.), *Toward a general theory of expertise* (pp. 301–336). Cambridge: Cambridge University Press.

Jacoby, L.L. (1978). On interpreting the effects of repetition: Solving a problem versus remembering a solution. In M.A. Quinones and A. Ehrenstein (eds.), *Training for a rapidly changing workplace: Applications of psychological research.* Washington, DC: American Psychological Association.

Johnson, C. (1998). The essential principles of action learning. *Journal of Workplace Learning, 10* (6/7), 296–300.

Kraiger, K., Ford, J.K. and Salas, E. (1993). Application of cognitive, skill-based, and affective theories of learning outcomes to new methods of training evaluation. *Journal of Applied Psychology, 78,* 311–28.

MacDonald, C.J., Gabriel, M.A. and Cousins, J.B. (2000). Factors influencing adult learning in technology based firms. *The Journal of Management Development, 19,* 220–40.

Mainemelis, C., Boyatzis, R. and Kolb, D.A. (2002). Learning styles and adaptive flexibility: Testing experiential learning theory. *Management Learning*, 33(1), 5–33.

Myers, G.L. and Fisk, A.D. (1987). Training consistent task components: Application of automatic and controlled processing theory to industrial task training. In M.A. Quinones and A. Ehrenstein (eds.), *Training for a rapidly changing workplace: Applications of psychological research*. Washington, DC: American Psychological Association.

Nadler, J., Thompson, L. and Van Boven, L. (2003). Learning negotiation skills: Four models of knowledge creation and transfer. *Management Science*, 49(4), 529–41.

Naylor, J.C. and Briggs, G.E. (1983). The effect of task complexity and task organization on the relative efficiency of part and whole training methods. *Journal of Experimental Psychology*, 65, 217–24.

Pedler, M. (1997). Interpreting action learning. In J. Burgoyne and M. Reynolds (Eds.), *Management Learning: Integrating Theory and Practice*. London: Sage.

Proctor, R.W. and Dutta, A. (1995). Skill acquisition and human performance. In M.A. Quinones and A. Ehrenstein (eds.), *Training for a rapidly changing workplace: Applications of psychological research*. Washington, DC: American Psychological Association.

Schmidt, R.A. and Bjork, R.A. (1992). New conceptualizations of practice: Common principles in three paradigms suggest new concepts for training. In J.K. Ford and D.A. Weissbein (1997), Transfer of training: An updated review and analysis. *Performance Improvement Quarterly*, 10(2), 22–41.

Schunk, D.H. (1996). *Learning theories. 2nd ed.* Englewood Cliffs, NJ: Prentice-Hall. In Z. Yildirim, M.Y. Ozden, and M. Aksu (2001), Comparison of hypermedia learning and traditional instruction on knowledge acquisition and retention. *The Journal of Educational Research*, 94(4), 207–20.

Shore, E. and Sechrest, L. (1961). Concept attainment as a function of positive instances presented. *Journal of Educational Psychology*, 52, 303–07.

Smith, P.A. and O'Neil, J. (2003a). A review of action learning literature 1994–2000: Part 1 – bibliography and comments. *Journal of Workplace Learning*, 15(2), 63–9.

Smith, P.A. and O'Neil, J. (2003b). A review of action learning literature 1994–2000: Part 2 – signposts into the literature. *Journal of Workplace Learning*, 15(4), 154–66.

Thompson, L., Gentner, D. and Lowenstein, J. (2000). Avoiding missed opportunities in managerial life: Analogical training more powerful than individual case training. *Organizational Behavior and Human Decision Processes*, 82(1), 60–75.

Smith, P.L. and Ragan, T.J. (1993). *Instructional design.* New York: Macmillan. In Z. Yildirim, M.Y. Ozden, and M. Aksu (2001), Comparison of hypermedia learning and traditional instruction on knowledge acquisition and retention. *The Journal of Educational Research,* 94(4), 207–20.

Thorndike, E.L. and Woodworth, R.S. (1901). The influence of improvement in one mental function upon the efficiency of other functions. In T.T. Baldwin and J.K. Ford (1988), Transfer of training: A review and directions for future research. *Personnel Psychology,* 41, 63–105.

Wills, G. and Oliver, C. (1996). Measuring the ROI from management action learning. *Management Development Review,* 9(1), 17–21.

Yorks, L., O'Neil, J., Marsick, V.J., Lamm, S., Kolodny, R. and Nilson, G. (1998). Transfer of learning from an action-reflection-learning program. *Performance Improvement Quarterly,* 11(1), 59–73.

# 3

# Bridging the Gap

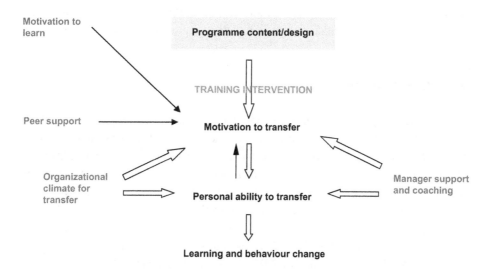

## Introduction

For effective learning transfer to happen, learners face two particular challenges. Firstly, however they achieve it, they must find the motivation to transfer what they have learned into meaningful changes in behaviour back at work. Secondly, they need somehow to find the time and the mental space to do so. This reflects their personal ability to transfer. Motivation and personal ability to transfer, along with the variety of conditions that influence them will be discussed more fully in Chapter 5. The factors relating to training content and design, seen in the previous chapter, exert their effect on learning transfer mainly through their effect on motivation to transfer. In this chapter, the emphasis will be on what can be done to help prepare the learner to overcome the challenges involved in the application of learning back at work. Thus the primary focus here will be the influence of a number of post-intervention activities on learners' personal ability to transfer.

For some, the gap between the comfortable, safe microcosm of the classroom and the often harsh reality of the workplace is one for which they are not well prepared. Confronting your overbearing boss may be fine in the practice of a role play but looks a lot scarier now that you're back at work. Or trying to remember all the steps involved (at the same time!) in closing a sale when confronted with real people and real money is not so easy. So, anything that helps bridge that gap should be welcomed. This chapter will discuss a number of techniques that do just that. These techniques are sometimes called 'post-training strategies', and are essentially supplemental training sessions, which don't add new skill content but rather focus on ways of sustaining skills learned in training. They include goal setting, relapse prevention, self-management and coaching.

## Setting Your Goals

Over the years, plenty of evidence has been gathered to suggest that setting clear goals to achieve specific ends makes achievement of those ends a more likely prospect. From losing weight to stopping smoking, from becoming a better tennis player to graduating with a degree, people have felt the benefits of setting out clearly what they want to do and how they are going to do it. Not surprisingly, the situation is the same with regard to the application of learning. From quite a while back, setting goals around the application of learning back at work has been demonstrated to have positive effects on the outcome (Wexley and Nemeroff 1975; Feldman 1981; Magjuka, Baldwin and Loher 1994). Sometimes also known as contracting, it is a process whereby some or all of the trainer, the trainee and the trainee's manager agree the achievement of certain application objectives by the trainee following training. The process may vary somewhat, although the intention is the same. For instance, following a leadership programme, participants might construct a checklist of behaviours to complete, such as giving feedback to an employee, or chairing a meeting, and would monitor and record their use of these new skills. Help in how to do this is often provided by the facilitator as part of the programme. While it's more common for participants to set their own goals (the 'participative' strategy), a variation on this is for the facilitator to actually decide the goals to be achieved (the 'assigned' strategy). Interestingly, a significant study undertaken by Wexley and Baldwin (1986) looked at both of these variations, and found that both the assigned and the participative goal-setting strategies resulted in significantly greater levels of maintenance of behaviour reported by trainees 2 months after the training took place. More recently, Brown and Latham (2000) examined the effects of goal setting and what they called 'self instruction' (this involves a short session at the end of the programme designed to raise participants' level of confidence in applying their learning) on transfer. On-the-job behaviour of the participants was measured 10 weeks after the programme by themselves and by their peers, using a behavioural observation scale. They discovered that if they included a 45-minute session at the end of the programme on the setting of specific goals, it was seen to be more effective in promoting transfer than not having such a session, and instead leaving it to participants to 'do their best'. This is a useful discovery as goal setting at the end of learning interventions is often quite a rushed affair, with little time for reflecting on how the goals will be achieved.

The way in which goal setting makes application of new learning more successful is the same as for any other endeavour. By making transfer objectives clear (sometimes publicly so) and by considering the ways in which they'll be

---

**BOX 3.1: SETTING SMART GOALS**

Sean works as a supervisor in the stores area for a medium-sized manufacturing company. Although he has worked for the company for quite a while, he has only recently been promoted to his current position. A personal development programme in which he participated has helped him to identify some priorities for himself, and he's now at the stage where he's trying to articulate some of his ideas into a goal. So far, all he can say is that he recognizes he'll have to get to know his four staff better, to better understand how to motivate them.

Deciding to use the SMART framework makes this easier for him. In terms of specificity, what does he mean by 'getting to know them better'? Some reflection on this with the help of the programme facilitator suggests to him that he needs to meet with them, and get them to do the talking about what they like, dislike and hope for with regard to their own jobs and working relationships. They agree this will be the agenda for the first meeting, and so he sets about deciding the questions he will ask. That takes care of specificity. Now he needs to decide whether the goal is measurable. Given that the goal has been specified as one meeting with each staff member, it will be easy to measure it, and to determine whether he has asked the questions he intended. As there are only four people and therefore four meetings involved, the goal is also actionable, and well within his capabilities. Some further reflection convinces him that it's also very relevant, as he feels this will improve his understanding of his staff members' perceptions about the job they do (and about himself as a boss) and thus provide the starting point for improving motivation and performance within the team. Finally, he puts a deadline of 1 month hence (realistic, given other demands on people's time) for the meetings to take place. Now all he has to do is start setting up the appointments.

achieved, usually through considerations around specificity, measurability and achievability, participants can construct a very clear view of what success in application looks like. The process of reflection that accompanies the setting of goals is also an important part of the process. Therefore, activities undertaken at the time of goal setting that encourage reflection should also improve the probability of them being achieved. For this reason, putting goals in writing and/or testing them with colleagues can also be helpful.

## Managing Yourself

In more recent times, studies on goal setting as a post-training strategy have dealt with it in the context of self-management, of which it is usually a component. In essence, self-management is concerned with encouraging trainees to consider as many issues as possible that might prevent their new skills or knowledge from surviving the transition from the training programme to the job, and to consider how they will deal with them. The intention is to enable them to cope with the realities of life back on-the-job, for example knowing how to react when they run into difficulty applying what they learned.

Where it differs from goal setting is that, in addition to actually setting some goals to achieve, a typical self-management session looks at how those goals might be achieved, what will get in the way of implementing them, what help will be needed and what help will be available. A short session incorporating these 'maintenance of behaviour' activities at the end of a programme has been shown to aid learning transfer. A particular piece of work in this regard by Gist, Bavetta and Stevens (1990) is interesting. Using negotiating skills programmes as the basis for their study, they compared a programme using a self-management session with one which used goal setting alone. What they found was that the self-management trainees achieved a higher level of transfer in negotiation simulations afterwards than did the goal setting trainees. Furthermore, the self-management trainees also used a broader range of negotiating strategies. In other words, when they encountered difficulty, they switched to a different strategy. On the other hand, the goal setting trainees were more likely to use the same strategies repeatedly, but put more effort into making them work. The researchers concluded that goal setting will be a more effective transfer strategy than self-management if effort is more important than skill in making transfer happen. Another piece of work, undertaken some years later by Richman-Hirsch (2001) would seem to suggest, however, that it is the goal setting component of self-management (recall that self-management strategies usually include some goal setting) that is the key. She conducted a study with 267 employees who had undergone training in customer service skills. As with the earlier study, goal setting and self-management were the post-training interventions applied, and their effects compared. Using responses from the trainees themselves and their colleagues, she found (unlike the earlier study) that goal setting had a greater effect on the post-training generalization of the skills learned than self-management. However, further analysis of the responses reveals that trainees in the study who were introduced to the self-management strategy were given very little specific instruction in setting goals. Thus both may need to work together for successful transfer.

In common with goal setting, the benefits of self-management are in the planning of what has to be done to facilitate application of learning following the programme, as well as identifying at an early stage what is likely to help or hinder that application. As with any plan, knowing what might 'get in the way', and indeed what help might be forthcoming enables an individual to be better prepared to meet the challenges posed.

---

**BOX 3.2: PREPARING FOR MONDAY**

A feature of the final day of a 3-day residential leadership development programme for managers in a large financial services organization is a session entitled 'Preparing for Monday'. The session, which lasts approximately 90 minutes, directly follows the session where participants complete their action plans. The action planning session itself is quite structured, and uses insights gained from the use of 180 degree instruments and self-assessment, as well as tutor input, case studies and role plays.

Following the construction of the action plan and its testing with another participant for specificity, relevance and the like, the session begins. Its purpose is to highlight and discuss barriers and supports to implementation of the action plan and application of learning from the programme back at work. Common barriers identified by participants usually include personal factors such as lack of assertiveness or autonomy, and organizational factors such as lack of line manager support, too many short-term priorities and lack of recognition of their efforts. They also receive guidance on how to handle the first meeting with staff on their return to work. The purpose of that particular meeting is to thank them for their feedback, summarize highlights and lowlights, and begin the process of behaviour change where appropriate. By the end of the session, participants have identified what is most likely to get in the way of them implementing their action plan, and have devised some strategies to be prepared for and tackle them. Whatever the challenges awaiting them back at work, at least they're leaving the programme with a high degree of confidence in their ability to cope with them.

## Preventing Relapse

Although it's a technique not far removed from those already discussed, some researchers have looked at the use of 'relapse prevention' as a way of improving learning transfer. Relapse prevention was originally used with addictive behaviours and is based on the model of Marlatt and Gordon (1980). The model proposes that anticipating and monitoring past and present failures will enhance long-term behaviour change. The individual then develops a response to cope with high-risk situations following the original intervention. Increased confidence following the successful overcoming of the high-risk situation decreases the probability of relapse. Marx (1982) was probably the first to investigate the use of the technique in management training. In this case, trainees discuss possible factors that are likely to inhibit their application of learned skills back on-the-job. In keeping with Marlatt and Gordon's model, it is hoped that having anticipated possible difficulties (perhaps their own lack of assertiveness or a work environment resistant to change) they are less likely to 'revert to type' under pressure when these situations arise. For example, studies by Burke (1997) and Burke and Baldwin (1999) examining the effect of relapse prevention training on the maintenance of learned knowledge and skills provide some support for its use, although this seems to depend on the transfer climate (a relapse prevention session may be of more value where the transfer climate is less supportive). The organizational climate for transfer will be discussed in Chapter 4.

## Action Planning

Interestingly, action planning as a specific activity has not received a lot of attention in the literature per se. This could be because it is in effect a composite of the activities already described – principally goal setting and self-management, which a comprehensive action plan is likely to contain. An action plan is really a statement of what the learner intends to do to enhance the chances of their learning translating into real changes in behaviour at work. While action plans can be constructed at any time, and don't even need to be part of a training or development event, it is usually such an event (and the reflective time that accompanies it) that starts the learning transfer process in earnest.

## Coaching: A Special Case

The practices and activities already described in this chapter are those that most often take place while the participants are still in the classroom, as it is often argued that it is the best (indeed sometimes the only) chance that they'll have to engage in reflection on what they have learned. However, the quest to find that elusive time to reflect on learning is being aided, particularly in the area of management development, by developments in the field of coaching.

As evidenced by the number and scope of coaching courses, qualifications and books now available, there has been a veritable explosion in the use of coaching for development in recent years. Some figures (Jarvis, Lane and Fillery-Travis 2006) put the value of the industry in the USA, for example, in excess of $500 million per annum, while other estimates suggest that there are of the order of 4000 professional coaches operating in the UK. Organizations and individuals are constantly being exhorted to become involved in coaching as a sure way of improving everything from their leadership to their love life. At the same time, it's becoming impossible to count the number of books hitting the shelves and e-retailers' websites that address the subject from every angle, and which continues to increase by the day.

Yet despite this, for such a popular topic, the amount of empirical research that has actually been conducted around coaching is disappointingly small. For instance Feldman and Lankau (2005) in a review of the literature, unearthed less than 20 studies that have investigated executive coaching systematically using quantitative or qualitative methods, while earlier, Kilburg (2000) found that the content of 14 books written on the topic since 1994 was based on only a dozen or so empirical studies. This lack of hard data will not help reduce the amount of cynicism amongst those who are not convinced of its efficacy, and see it as the current 'flavour of the month'. Perhaps they have reasons to be cynical. A recent survey by the Chartered Institute of Personnel and Development (CIPD, 2006) indicated that 34 per cent of respondents felt that 'lack of belief in the value of coaching' is a barrier to coaching activity. In the same survey, 42 per cent believed a lack of data to prove the value of coaching activities to also be a drawback. There is also a strong body of opinion, including Berglas (2002) which suggests that the popularity of coaching has a lot to do with a demand amongst the business community for quick solutions, preferably delivered as painlessly as possible.

## So, What is Coaching?

Coaching is usually described in terms of it being a practical, goal-focused form of personal one-to-one learning (Hall, Otazo and Hollenbeck 1999). It typically

---

**BOX 3.3: COACHING USING A BEHAVIOURIST APPROACH**

David is a manager who has realized he's not exactly a world beater when it comes to giving feedback to staff on their performance. He seems to waver between the two extremes of either being too blunt or not being clear enough, with obvious consequences for the effectiveness of the message he's trying to convey. His coach Bill has suggested a simple model for giving feedback for him to practise. Called BeCA, it focuses on the *behaviour* that's inappropriate, the *consequences* of that behaviour and the *action* required. He has been asked to try this out at least three times before his next coaching session.

He prepares a script which will guide him throughout the conversation he's about to have. He's decided on a relatively easy one to start, a case of a new staff member whose report writing contains an unacceptably large number of spelling errors. He's a little nervous, although he did try out this conversation in role-play with Bill at the last session. He's been thinking about all the possible responses the staff member might come up with, but has been told by Bill just to focus on the model – highlight the behaviour that's inappropriate (the typing errors), state the consequences (the image of his department, the amount of rework needed) before moving on to the desired action (use a spellchecker or get someone else to look at it). At least the three steps will focus his mind, and if it doesn't work there's always the next coaching session. It works. Not quite how he expected it to, but it gives him sufficient confidence to use it again for the next conversation. He's now thinking, 'Perhaps this feedback thing is not so difficult after all.'

---

takes the form of a short- to medium-term relationship between a manager or executive and a coach or consultant, in order to improve the effectiveness of the former. While the focus of and process by which coaching achieves its aims varies, coaching interventions usually comprise three main elements – one-to-one counselling about work-related issues; use of 360-degree feedback on strengths and development areas as a starting point; and a focus on the improvement of effectiveness in the (executive's) current job (Feldman 2001). For the purposes of this chapter, the discussion on coaching will be taken to mean what has become widely known as executive coaching, that is, the use of an external coach whose sole responsibility is to help executives improve their performance (the role of one's own manager as a coach will be discussed in Chapter 4). Although the intended role of an executive coach is quite clear, the process should be a collaborative one, involving the coach, the manager and their boss.

As the subject of coaching in general is more than adequately dealt with in a variety of other publications, the focus here will be on the role of coaching as a learning transfer tool. Interestingly, coaching doesn't get discussed much in the literature in the context of learning transfer. Perhaps it may be that coaching for transfer involves the development of a personal ability to transfer, a process that involves goal setting, collaborative problem solving, practice and feedback, and supervisory involvement (Olivero, Bane and Kopelman 1997), factors that are also components of other learning transfer strategies. They have already been or will be discussed in other chapters. In any event, the emphasis in this section will not be so much on *whether* coaching works (the evidence clearly suggests it does) but more on *how* it works, as this is important to understand in the context of its role in facilitating learning transfer.

## What Does the Literature Say?

What literature there is has dealt with the subject from a number of angles, including the demographic backgrounds (Judge and Cowell 1997) and credentials (Garman, Whiston and Zlatoper 2000; Wasylyshyn 2003) of effective coaches. However, it is the research into the outcomes and perceived effectiveness of coaching that we'll focus on here.

One of the earlier studies cited (Olivero, Bane and Kopelman 1997) involved 31 managers undergoing a management training programme, which was followed by individual coaching over a period of 8 weeks. The researchers found that training alone increased productivity by 22 per cent. However, when the coaching component (which included a number of the elements mentioned above as well as an evaluation of the end-results and a public presentation) is included the overall gain in productivity was 88 per cent. They attribute this very sizeable gain largely to the motivational effect of feedback received from achievement of goals by the protégés (as coachees or clients are sometimes called) and its effect on their self-efficacy (in other words, confidence in their ability to achieve their goals). In another study, Hall, Otazo and Hollenbeck (1999) also interviewed 75 managers participating in executive coaching. Their respondents reported learning and changes in behaviour as a result of coaching, and rated the overall effectiveness of the coaching programme very highly. Two other studies, undertaken in 2001, also indicate positive outcomes. Kampa-Kokesch (2001), although her methodology might be open to criticism, reported that 75 per cent of executives felt that the coaching programme they engaged in had added value that was significantly greater than the time and money invested. The other (Sloan 2001) looked at coaching as an additional intervention to a formal programme. While conducting research involving executive education programmes, she found that participants working with a coach or mentor before or after their programme, or both, reported greater self-confidence, and greater skill in developing others, than those who did not.

Finally, two other studies since 2000 have also found positive transfer effects for coaching interventions. Thach (2002) found that multi-rater feedback combined with individual coaching increased the leadership effectiveness of the participants (as measured by peers and direct reports) by up to 60 per cent. And Smither et al. (2003) discovered that managers who worked with an executive coach were more likely to set specific goals, solicit ideas for improvement from supervisors and receive improved ratings from direct reports and supervisors.

## How Does it Work?

The above results paint a very positive picture of the beneficial effects of coaching. It appears that for individuals, generating confidence in their ability to achieve goals makes an important contribution. So too does the setting of those goals. However, missing from the above success stories is an indication of how the process of coaching helps with behaviour change and the implementation of new ideas back at work. Perhaps one way to examine this is to take a look at some of the approaches executive coaches use.

## Different Approaches

The huge growth in the practice of coaching alluded to earlier has drawn practitioners into the profession from a range of backgrounds. At one end of the spectrum, some coaches have backgrounds in counselling psychology and therapy, perhaps having built up experience dealing with 'troubled' individuals in clinical settings. At the deepest level, their experience will probably have involved attempting to gain access to their client's unconscious thoughts, given that these may be driving particular behaviours or distorted perceptions. In coaching, therefore, the approach they take may favour trying to increase the client's self-awareness of their thoughts and feelings. At the other end of the spectrum, coaches may be just putting their practical experience of managing and developing others into operation. Their coaching approaches do not probe so deeply, but nevertheless help the client understand the links between their thought processes and their behaviour, with a view to getting them to take responsibility for the outcome. Each may also make use of input provided from

---

**BOX 3.4: COACHING USING A COGNITIVE APPROACH**

Alan has just undergone a 3-day development programme for experienced team leaders with management potential like himself. One of the items of interest he has taken away from the programme is a sense that none of the other team leaders on the programme (it was an open programme, and participants were drawn from a range of organizations) seem to know any more about managing people than he does. In fact he would reckon he has greater insights than they do. Why is it then, that he is very nervous about applying for an upcoming vacancy, convincing himself he needs more time in his current role before he's ready? Luckily for him, the programme also entails 8 hours of coaching as part of the learning support offered, to help him translate what he learns from the classroom to the office.

Throughout the coaching process, his coach Emma encourages him to think through reasons why he feels he's 'not ready'. He's not sure himself at first, but Emma's skill in getting him to articulate what's in his mind gradually draws out his underlying perceptions concerning issues such as the specific demands of the job advertised, as well as his perceptions concerning his own capability to perform at that level. For example, he initially felt he didn't have enough operational experience for the job, but came to realize that gaps in his CV were matched by equally large gaps in those of other likely contenders. In addition, through the use of appropriate probing questions, his coach helped him to see the relevance of some of the qualifications and unique experience he possessed, something he hadn't really thought about before. As a result, he gradually develops a sufficient level of confidence in his ability to perform the job, and decides he'll give it a go. At the very least, he'll raise his profile in the department and remind those who matter that he has a lot to offer.

---

those around the client – peers, boss or staff – in order to raise the level of awareness and begin the process of behaviour change.

It is highly unlikely in the pragmatic world of business that one approach will provide all the answers, and so it is common to see elements of different approaches in the same process. In Chapter 1 we defined two principal approaches to learning in the workplace – the behaviourist approach, which focuses on observable behaviour, and the cognitive approach, which looks at what's going on inside the learner's head. In practice, most coaching involves elements from and some degree of overlap between these two approaches, although the starting points may be different. A cognitive approach to coaching is most likely to facilitate learning transfer by changing the way a client views a particular difficulty or set of circumstances. On the other hand, behaviourist approaches encourage the client to consider the causes and consequences of their behaviour. So, whether starting from inside the client's head and working out, or starting with the client's behaviour and working in, coaches use the insights provided from these processes to increase self-awareness and generate a desire to change particular behaviours.

## A Question of Time and Space

Recall that the role for coaching in which we're particularly interested here is its role in helping to create the time and mental space for individuals to reflect upon and change their thinking and behaviour. Many of the behaviours that successful coaches engage in do just that. In creating that time and space, they first spend time developing a rapport with the client. This acknowledges the need to 'step back' mentally from the work, establish trust, empathy and confidence in the coach's credentials. Only when this has been achieved can the substantive work begin. The fact that coaching often takes place outside the normal physical work environment facilitates the creation of space to think. The second way in which coaching can help create the space is the way in which an effective coach will encourage the client to think through the issues under consideration. This is usually achieved by asking appropriate questions to elicit facts, opinions and feelings, and reflecting and summarizing to help clients clarify for themselves what's on their mind. Thirdly, good coaches help the client identify options, perhaps broadening the client's perspective and getting them to see things in a different way. They can also challenge the client's thinking if they see that as a barrier to behaviour change.

There is also an increasing trend, mostly well founded, to use feedback instruments as part of the process. There are many such instruments, available from a range of providers. Appropriate use of these instruments will of course depend on the circumstances and the objectives of the coaching. Ultimately, however, they can help learning transfer by providing objective information to support perceptions from other sources, and thus stimulate real thinking on the client's strengths and opportunities for development.

## In Practice

For a high proportion of training and development programmes, any control the programme facilitator has over the amount of learning that takes place usually comes to an end when the group breaks up on the final day. Therefore that day may be the facilitator's last opportunity to influence the application of learning back at work. They should use it by including or encouraging at least some of the 'bridging' activities discussed in this section. If coaching has been built in, or indeed if coaching is an intervention in itself, the suggestions provided will increase the chances of real behaviour change at work taking place.

## PROMOTE GOAL SETTING (AND GIVE SUFFICIENT TIME TO IT ON THE PROGRAMME)

Unfortunately, for many training programmes, the action planning session, if one exists, is the few minutes at the end of the programme where the trainers can be tidying up the room while trainees try to think up excuses why they really should make a move now in order to catch that train and anyhow they'll have more time to think about it when they get home... This is perhaps not helped either by certain types of trainers who feel that once they've stopped talking the programme is over. Yet, the evidence clearly shows that even a small investment of time will generate at least some degree of benefit. The most tried and trusted method for setting learning goals is probably still the SMART method. Making goals as specific, measurable, actionable, relevant and timed as possible will greatly enhance the possibility of their being achieved.

The amount of time given to goal setting will no doubt vary with the length of the programme. A short workshop on a specific topic may complete the process in a matter of minutes. Longer programmes, where more complex skills and knowledge are involved or where feedback needs to be reflected upon, should allow significantly longer. In these situations, one-to-one assistance with goal setting can also be of benefit.

## HAVE PARTICIPANTS CONSTRUCT AN ACTION PLAN

Writing down what one intends to achieve is the first step in meeting the commitment. Experience has shown that the most effective action plans typically follow a thought process something like the following:

- Participants should start by taking a few minutes to think about what has been learned during the programme, considering inputs from the facilitators and other participants, discussions around the table, exercises and case studies.

- They should identify areas in which success is already being achieved as well as areas in which improvements might be made. The key is to choose areas that are important to them and to the performance of their unit/team, and where they feel that their efforts can have a beneficial impact. It is also important to focus on specific behaviours they wish to demonstrate rather than thinking about their attitudes or personality (it is far easier to change behaviour). In considering the areas in which to make improvements, they should be advised not to attempt to tackle more than two or three areas, on the basis that setting too many goals will more likely result in no goals being achieved. For each improvement action, participants can ask themselves the questions below to serve as a support for the thinking process:
  - What is the benefit of taking action?
  - What are the consequences of not taking action?
  - What is my objective for this 'area for action'? (remember SMART)
  - What are the obstacles to achieving my objective?
  - How will I know if I am succeeding?
  - What help will I need to achieve my objective?

- An additional benefit can be gained by discussing the draft action plan with a colleague, perhaps a fellow participant on the programme. The role of that individual can be to 'reality test' the plan for its specificity, measurability or achievability. Changes to be made to the plan can be noted there and then.

## CONDUCT A SELF-MANAGEMENT SESSION AT THE END OF THE PROGRAMME

Any self-management session is likely to include some goal setting, as described above. However, an extra step can be introduced once participants have outlined a plan and discussed it with a course colleague. The facilitator may wish to introduce a session in which participants consider what faces them in terms of implementing their action plan when they get back to work, and how they might be able to deal with it. Typically this session discusses (in plenary) issues such as how specifically changes in behaviour will be made, where resistance might come from, what they'll need from their manager, and so on – in essence this is 'relapse prevention'.

## ENCOURAGE PARTICIPANTS TO MEET WITH THEIR MANAGER

While the influence training providers can have on participants after the programme is limited, they should nevertheless strongly encourage participants to meet with their manager soon after their return to work. It is crucial in terms of 'closing the loop' begun with the pre-programme meeting. The action plan can provide the starting point for this meeting. How it will be implemented, what support is available, and what barriers need to be surmounted should all be on the agenda. As we'll see in Chapter 5, the support of participants' managers is regularly identified as an essential element in helping to generalize and maintain new knowledge and learned skills in the workplace. In this regard, managers who are skilled in coaching are in a position to be of most help. In the real world, of course, many managers (usually those who see training and development as 'someone else's job') would rather not get involved in the process, so in those circumstances the participant should be encouraged to take the initiative.

## HOLD FOLLOW-UP/PROBLEM-SOLVING SESSIONS

Having a clear and specific action plan to implement is a good starting point for transferring learning back to work. In order to maintain focus on its completion, experience has shown that arranging a date for participants to meet again, several weeks after their last attendance, can be useful. In many cases, the primary objective of these get-togethers is to review action plan successes and failures, and provide feedback and support. They can also be used to refresh previous learning points, or indeed present new ones. They may even be used to develop new action plans. Sessions like these are increasingly being built in to development programmes. A typical arrangement is where training providers incorporate the first of these as part of the programme, and then promote the benefits of continuing the practice.

## ENCOURAGE PARTICIPANTS TO MAINTAIN CONTACT WITH EACH OTHER

A major benefit participants very often report from programmes is the opportunity to form networks with people who have to deal with similar issues. Keeping in touch with those who attended the same programme has a number of advantages. Firstly, in the context of the action plan, pairs of participants may exchange plans and undertake to monitor each other's progress, providing timely reminders of promises made. They can also act as sounding boards or sources of advice for each other with regard to difficulties that arise. Aside from the specifics of the action plan, small groups (perhaps from the same location or the same type of work environment) may decide to meet for lunch or coffee to provide mutual support and challenge. However, rather than leave the possibility of networking to chance (participants' actions don't always match their good intentions!) it is usually possible to set up these networks before they depart from the programme.

## ENCOURAGE PARTICIPANTS TO MONITOR THEIR OWN BEHAVIOUR FOLLOWING THE PROGRAMME

Even if participants haven't actually set out an action plan or chosen some specific goals to achieve, a little monitoring of their own behaviour back at work will still prove useful in helping them incorporate their new learning into their work. It may involve them in such actions as:

- setting (small) goals;

- initiating particular behaviour changes (for example, planning a communication differently);

- looking out for opportunities to apply new learning (such as conducting a feedback session or chairing a meeting).

## ENCOURAGE PARTICIPANTS TO REVIEW THE CONTENT

If for no other reason than to bring issues, frameworks and techniques discussed on the programme from the back of their minds to the front, participants should be encouraged to set aside a small amount of time at regular intervals to review course materials. Even something like half an hour per month for 6 months would pay dividends. It's not at all uncommon for such trawls to unearth something that didn't have an application at the time or that sparks off a relevant and useful train of thought. Diary dates for these reviews can even be set before participants leave the programme. Experience also suggests that where course handouts have been practical, participants refer to them.

## SUGGEST THAT PARTICIPANTS DEVELOP A MENTORING RELATIONSHIP

Mentors can be a rich source of information, experience and guidance. Participants should be encouraged to consider approaching someone they know who would be happy to take on the role. If the use of mentoring as part of the programme is being considered, then some input can be provided as to how to gain the most from it. Of course in some cases mentoring may already be happening informally, and this should be taken into account, rather than 'forcing' another process on participants.

## CONSIDER USING AN EXECUTIVE COACH

The explosion in the level of coaching activity alluded to earlier has brought with it some bad practice as well as good. Yet if chosen correctly, an effective coach – one skilled in listening, problem solving, and with an understanding of human dynamics, amongst other qualities – can be of great assistance to an individual in identifying and meeting a variety of development needs. On the surface, coaching is an expensive option, and for this reason tends to be undertaken with those at higher levels in organizations. Yet the significant investment of time (and thus money) involved should be balanced against what the evidence seems to suggest are equally significant learning and performance outcomes. Coaching interventions have the benefit of dealing with specific issues relating to specific situations, as well as being very flexible in terms of how they're conducted. In this way, both learning and learning transfer are taking place at the same time.

## BE CLEAR ABOUT THE PURPOSE OF THE COACHING

Given what has already been said about the importance of a clear training or development needs analysis, what is expected from the coaching process needs to be established early on in that process. The development of rapport between coach and client is an important first step. For the client, it's an opportunity to understand the coach's background and experience, and get a sense of their approach. For the coach, it's an opportunity to identify the issues the client is dealing with (or not dealing with as the case may be) and decide whether they might be in a position to help.

If they are in such a position, then both can move on to setting some goals for the intervention. In reality, it's not always possible to be clear from the outset on what those goals might be. It's not unheard of for coaching interventions to begin with an 'open agenda' approach, while together the coach and client start to explore, in an unstructured way, issues such as the client's feelings, hopes or motivations. While working in this way can uncover useful background information, it is not usually the way in which coaching interventions work.

Once the issues have been highlighted, it is usually more effective to start providing some clarity (that is, set some goals) around how they will be dealt with in the process.

## DECIDE WHETHER IT SHOULD STAND ALONE OR AS PART OF SOMETHING ELSE

For some decision makers, the choice presented is sometimes whether to go with a training or development programme on the one hand, with its advantages of building effective teams or spreading knowledge through the organization more quickly, and an individually-focused intervention, such as coaching on the other. What is increasingly happening in practice is a combining of these two approaches, in order to achieve the best of both worlds. We saw in Chapter 2 that meeting with others, sharing experience and questioning assumptions with people in both similar and different situations have already been promoted as effective ways of transferring learning. Yet we also saw that in addition to this, having the time and the mental space to think through issues raised, as well as a real opportunity to try them out in practice with guided support can really make the likelihood of new behaviour 'sticking' much greater.

In practice, experience suggests that the two processes can operate very effectively in parallel, particularly with longer programmes delivered over a period of time. Many development programmes now offer a number of hours of coaching support (between 5 and 10 hours is quite typical) as an opportunity for participants to receive help in personalizing learning objectives from the programme, and guidance in turning their motivation to transfer into reality. Indeed group follow-up sessions, scheduled after a number of coaching sessions have taken place, can further help consolidate learning.

## USE AS MANY SOURCES OF INFORMATION AS POSSIBLE

A good coach will make it easier for clients to clarify and better understand their own strengths and areas for development. Yet the client is only one source of data. Depending on the client and the intervention, relevant data may be available from a number of other sources. If a client manages others, their input on how they do so will provide a range of perceptions that together paint a picture of what happens in reality. The client's boss is another source. They will have yet a different viewpoint, particularly if their focus is on the client's outputs rather than how they are achieved. If appropriate, customers can also contribute.

Data from these sources can be gathered in a number of ways. The use of 360 degree-type instruments, particularly in the context of measuring behaviours or competencies is popular and, depending on the instruments, also valid and reliable. However this data may also be available from interview reports, assessment or development centres and customer feedback.

## BUILD EVALUATION INTO THE COACHING PROCESS FROM THE START

As with any learning intervention, being clear about what a coaching intervention is intended to achieve is a must, in order for it to be effective. Demonstrating its effectiveness will go a long way towards allaying fears that coaching is an expensive luxury, with uncertain outcomes. That is why the ways in which effectiveness will be monitored and measured need to be in place at the outset, in order to maintain the effort and direction of the process. Pre- and post-coaching measures such as scores on competency or behavioural profiles, achievement of targets set, as well as personal reflections can all provide evidence in this regard.

## Summary

In summary, the evidence clearly suggests that goal setting is an effective post-training strategy in facilitating transfer from training programmes. While support for relapse prevention as a transfer tool is mixed, self-management activities have been shown to be effective. However, as all the transfer strategies discussed contain goal setting as a component, there is clearly a relationship between them. Furthermore, it appears that goal setting itself is a central part of the process for effective learning transfer. It would seem that the key to transfer is around making conscious decisions about how the training will be used, and anticipating difficulties and generating strategies to cope with them in order to transfer learning. Finally, as a particular example of post-training intervention (or indeed as a 'bridging' activity in its own right), coaching has received much attention, although much more in applied settings than in empirical studies. Nevertheless, what empirical evidence is available appears to support its positive effect on learning transfer through facilitating goal setting, collaborative problem solving, practice and feedback, and the building up of sufficient confidence to make the necessary changes.

## References

Berglas, S. (2002). The very real dangers of executive coaching. *Harvard Business Review*, 80, 86–93.

Brown, T.C. and Latham, G.P. (2000). The effects of goal setting and self-instruction training on the performance of unionized employees. *Relations Industrielles*, 55(1), 80–95.

Burke, L.A. (1997). Improving positive transfer: A test of relapse prevention training on transfer outcomes. *Human Resource Development Quarterly*, 8(2), 115–28.

Burke, L.A. and Baldwin, T.T. (1999). Workforce training transfer: A study of the effects of relapse prevention training and transfer climate. *Human Resource Management*, 38(3), 227–41.

CIPD (2006). *Learning and Development 2006,* Survey Report, London: CIPD. http://www.cipd.co.uk/surveys. Accessed 10 June 2008.

Feldman, D.C. (2001). Career coaching: What HR professionals and managers need to know. *Human Resource Planning*, 24, 26–35.

Feldman, D.C. and Lankau, M.J. (2005). Executive coaching: A review and agenda for further research. *Journal of Management*, 31(6), 829–48.

Feldman, M. (1981). Successful post-training skill application. *Training and Development Journal*, 35, 72–5.

Garman, A.N., Whiston, D.L. and Zlatoper, K.W. (2000). Media perceptions of executive coaching and the formal preparation of coaches. *Consulting Psychology Journal: Practice and Research*, 52, 201–05.

Gist, M.E., Bavetta, A.G. and Stevens, C.K. (1990). Transfer training methods: Its influence on skill generalization, skills repetition, and performance level. *Personnel Psychology*, 43, 501–23.

Hall, D.T., Otazo, K.L. and Hollenbeck, G.P. (1999). Behind closed doors: What really happens in executive coaching. *Organizational Dynamics*, 27(3), 39–52.

Jarvis, J., Lane, D.A. and Fillery-Travis, A. (2006). *The case for coaching: Making evidence-based decisions.* London: CIPD.

Judge, W.Q. and Cowell, J. (1997). The brave new world of executive coaching. *Business Horizons*, 40, 71–7.

Kampa-Kokesch, S. (2001). *Executive coaching as an individually tailored consultation intervention: Does it increase leadership?* Unpublished doctoral dissertation, Western Michigan University.

Kilburg, R.R. (2000). *Executive coaching: Developing managerial wisdom in a world of chaos.* Washington, DC: American Psychological Association. In K. Kraiger (ed.), *Creating, implementing, and managing effective training and development: State-of-the-art lessons for practice.* San Francisco: Jossey-Bass.

Magjuka, R., Baldwin, T.T. and Loher, B.T. (1994). The combined effects of three pretraining strategies on motivation and performance: An empirical exploration. *Journal of Managerial Issues*, 6(3), 282–96.

Marlatt, G.A. and Gordon, J.R. (1980). Determinants of relapse: Implications for the maintenance of behavior change. In R.D. Marx (1982), Relapse prevention for managerial training: A model for maintenance of behavior change. *Academy of Management Review*, 7, 433–41.

Marx, R.D. (1982). Relapse prevention for managerial training: A model for maintenance of behavior change. *Academy of Management Review*, 7, 433–41.

Olivero, G., Bane, D.K. and Kopelman, R.E. (1997). Executive coaching as a transfer of training tool: Effects on productivity in a public agency. *Public Personnel Management*, 26(4), 461–69.

Richman-Hirsch, W.L. (2001). Post-training interventions to enhance transfer: The moderating effects of work environments. *Human Resource Development Quarterly*, 12(2), 105–20.

Sloan, E.B. (2001). *The contribution of university-based executive education to corporate executive talent management results.* Joint research project conducted by the international university consortium for executive education (UNICON) and Personnel Decisions International. Minneapolis: Personnel Decisions International. In K. Kraiger (ed.), *Creating, implementing, and managing effective training and development: State-of-the-art lessons for practice.* San Francisco: Jossey-Bass.

Smither, J.W., London, M., Flautt, R., Vargas, Y. and Kucine, I. (2003). Can working with an executive coach improve multisource feedback ratings? A quasi-experimental field study. *Personnel Psychology*, 56(1), 23–44.

Thach, E.C. (2002). The impact of executive coaching and 360 feedback on leadership effectiveness. *Leadership and Organization Development Journal*, 23, 205–21.

Wasylyshyn, K.M. (2003). Executive coaching: An outcome study. *Consulting Psychology Journal: Practice and Research*, 55, 94–106.

Wexley, K.N. and Baldwin, T.T. (1986). Post-training strategies for facilitating positive transfer: An empirical exploration. *Academy of Management Journal*, 29, 503–20.

Wexley, K.N. and Nemeroff, W. (1975). Effectiveness of positive reinforcement and goal setting as methods of management development. *Journal of Applied Psychology*, 64, 239–46.

# 4

# Getting the Work Environment Right

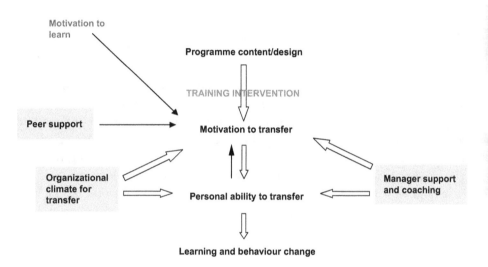

## Introduction

This chapter will deal with conditions specific to the work environment from which trainees come to training and to which they will return after the event. For the purposes of this chapter, the work environment factors that help or hinder learning transfer can be attributed to the presence or absence of support from three sources – peers, the organization in general and, most importantly, the trainee's manager. Peer support refers to the extent to which those around the trainee reinforce and support the use of learning on-the-job. It includes behaviours such as being open to ideas brought back from a learning event, giving feedback on the use of new learning, and in general, giving the benefit of their own learning and experience in a positive way. Support for learning from the organization can take a number of forms. A lack of undue constraints in performing one's job is one of them. The organization's openness in terms of communication and the general ease or otherwise with which new things can be done is another. Support from a training participant's manager is perhaps the most crucial, and can be provided in many ways. Examples include discussion of training needs and outcomes before and after attendance at an event, setting performance goals, as well as the empowerment of the individual to apply what they've learned without undue interference. Given their critical role in facilitating learning transfer, the constituent factors will be discussed in some detail in this chapter. They will be discussed first in the context of their combined effect, and later in terms of particular effects they have on transfer.

## What the Literature Says

The literature has quite a lot to say on organizational climates and learning transfer, as over the years, there has been a significant amount of management research undertaken on the subject. This research has tended to focus on climate in particular settings, such as climate for learning, climate for innovation and so on, and tried to relate these to specific dependent measures, such as learning transfer. In many ways, the sum total of effects on learning transfer from managers, peers and the organization in general creates what could be described as a 'climate for transfer', in which these various and interacting effects create a set of conditions that will help or hinder application of new learning.

## A Climate for Transfer

Although it has been called by different names over the years, the subject of transfer climate has been looked at by researchers for quite a while. It has also been known as environmental favourability (Noe 1986); organizational climate for innovation (Huczynski and Lewis 1980) and learning climate (Yorks et al. 1998). Essentially a transfer climate is a set of employee perceptions concerning what in the work environment helps or hinders them in their application of learning. Factors can include attitudes of supervisors and co-workers, workload, company policies, the level of job stress or the pace of change in the work unit. Transfer climate therefore refers to different but related aspects of the organizational environment to which trainees return following a training intervention. The consensus is that more helpful climates result in greater learning transfer.

The idea is not new, and a number of large-scale studies over the years have looked at a range of factors in the work environment that can help, or in many cases, hinder the application of learning. Some of these are outlined in Table 4.1. The earliest of them, from Baumgartel and JeanPierre (1972) concluded that the climate effect is itself partly a consequence of a set of complex interactions among work environment factors, individual trainee characteristics and training programme design factors. They found six aspects of organizational climates that correlated most strongly with reported efforts by trainees of their intention to apply their learning. What's interesting is that all of the factors identified seem to be just as relevant today. For the record, they were:

- the freedom to set personal performance goals;

- the degree to which higher management is considerate of the feelings of lower management;

- the degree to which the organization stimulates and approves of innovation and experimentation;

- the degree to which the organization is anxious for executives to make use of knowledge gained in management courses;

- the degree of free and open communication among the management group;

- the willingness of top management to spend money on training.

A short time later Huczynski (1977) described his 'climate for innovation' in terms of nine characteristics broadly similar to those above, such as how prepared the organization is to try out new things and take risks, how much people are allowed to 'get on with the job' themselves, and the degree to which authority can be questioned.

Since then, most of the work done appears to have dealt with the same dimensions, and has come to broadly similar conclusions regarding what conditions most affect learning transfer. Noe (1986), for instance, suggested that 'environmental favourability' comprises two elements – task favourability and social favourability. The former relates to trainees' perceptions concerning the availability of such supports as equipment, materials and financial resources, and will affect the degree to which new knowledge and skills will be used. The

**Table 4.1     Studies on learning transfer climate**

| Baumgartel and Jeanpierre (1972) | Huczynski (1977) | Rouiller and Goldstein (1993) |
|---|---|---|
| Freedom to set performance goals | Readiness to innovate | Situational cues<br>• Goal cues |
|  | Future orientation | • Social cues |
| The degree to which higher management is considerate of the feelings of lower management | Open mindedness | • Task cues<br>• Self-control cues |
|  | Rewards | Consequences of application<br>• Positive feedback |
| The degree to which the organization stimulates and approves of innovation and experimentation | Questioning of authority | • Negative feedback<br>• Punishment |
|  | Functions of conflict | • No feedback |
|  | Superior's attitude |  |
| The degree to which the organization is anxious for executives to make use of knowledge gained on management courses | Organizational structure |  |
|  | Responsibility, trust and support |  |
| The degree of free and open communication among the management group |  |  |
| The willingness of top management to spend money for training |  |  |

latter relates to perceptions regarding the opportunity to use that knowledge and skill, and the degree of feedback and support from others in the work group. This characteristic, according to Noe, affects transfer through the trainees' motivation to learn, and their motivation to transfer. Both motivation to learn and motivation to transfer will be discussed in Chapter 5.

Other work since has shown up many of the same results (Rouiller and Goldstein 1993; Tracey, Tannenbaum and Kavanagh 1995; Yorks et al. 1998; Bennett, Lehman and Forst 1999; Awoniyi, Griego and Morgan 2002, Clarke 2002). All have variously found effects for transfer climate in terms of trainee motivation, opportunities to use what they learned, the influence of workload and the trainee's job autonomy. Not surprisingly, they found that more helpful climates resulted in greater transfer. Results from the two most recent studies cited, both published in 2002, show remarkable similarity in terms of the organizational climate areas that are seen to have the greatest effect on learning transfer. They are summarized in Table 4.2.

Table 4.2        Organizational climate influences on learning transfer

| Clarke 2002 | Awoniyi, Griego and Morgan 2002 |
|---|---|
| Transfer is inhibited where individuals' (heavy) workloads are a barrier to reflecting on and trying out new skills | Transfer is facilitated if supervisors encourage and support subordinates, communicate effectively and set clear expectations and goals |
| Transfer is inhibited where deadlines and the urgent nature of many tasks leave little time for learning new ways of doing things, or reflecting on that learning | Transfer is facilitated if sufficient resources such as access to appropriate facilities, equipment, funds and information are available |
| Transfer is inhibited if trainees do not receive regular feedback on their efforts to apply new learning from those in their work environment | Transfer is facilitated if employees have the freedom to decide how to accomplish tasks and have a sense of control over their work and ideas |
| Transfer is inhibited if supervisors do not support, encourage or reward the use of new skills or knowledge at work | Transfer is inhibited if there is too much workload pressure such as unrealistic expectations, insufficient time and distractions |
| Transfer is inhibited if the training is not seen as directly useful in the trainee's current job | Transfer is facilitated if there is support for creativity in the work environment |

## The Components of Climate for Transfer

What's interesting from the above is that in many of the studies cited, barriers to transfer have tended to be mentioned with much greater frequency than supports. Perhaps this is an indication that typical work environments are not great places for learning transfer to happen. If that is so, then a deeper understanding of what actually is going on in work environments to help or hinder the transfer process would be useful, and provide a focus for interventions aimed at improving them. For that reason, we'll take a look at the elements that make up a climate for transfer as we discussed earlier – support from peers, support from the organization in general and support from the trainee's manager.

## Support From Your Peers

The importance of peer support (the extent to which peers reinforce and support the use of learning on-the-job) in helping the application of learning back at work has been documented in a number of studies. Peers may either be co-attendees on a programme or colleagues at work. Evidence for the benefit of peer support in the workplace exists, but is not overwhelming. Work by some researchers (Roullier and Goldstein 1993; Tracey, Tannenbaum and Kavanagh 1995) has pointed to its role as a component of a learning transfer climate. However, it seems that where peer support in facilitating learning transfer can be far more powerful is where peers are co-attendees on a programme. The benefits of mutual feedback and reinforcement amongst participants, discussed in previous chapters, are widely accepted. Where they come together, as in an action learning programme, the effect can be very positive. Recall that in action learning, the learning is occurring in the workplace rather than outside it. On top of that, if peers are also collaborators in the learning process, then many of the problems of transfer are circumvented (Yorks et al. 1998; Smith and O'Neil 2003a, 2003b).

## HOW IT WORKS

With regard to colleagues at work, peer support can manifest itself in different ways. Within the work environment for example, this might be demonstrated in a general enthusiasm for change, an interest in what the attendee had learned on the training programme and a willingness to try new ways of doing things. Supportive peers will listen, question and openly discuss issues that arose from the training. They will give feedback, both positive and critical, on attempts to

---

**BOX 4.1: LACK OF OPPORTUNITY TO USE LEARNING**

Michael is a little bit frustrated. As part of his company's graduate development programme he's been told he has to attend a 2-day workshop next month on how to manage teams. All the people at his level are required to attend in order to be considered for promotion to the next level. He's a great believer in learning but would rather this came at another time. In particular, given that he's an audit specialist and doesn't have a team to manage he feels his time would be better spent for example updating himself on new fraud legislation, which has important implications for his job. Nevertheless, being a good 'company man' Michael goes along.

The workshop is interesting, and raises a lot of issues that Michael sees will be important to him when he has a team to manage. He completed an action plan at the workshop, but it was more about dealing with colleagues, and not of direct relevance. In addition, his manager hasn't had any input into how the learning from the workshop might be useful. So he does what countless others before him have done. He leaves the folder with the expensively-acquired notes on the bookshelf in his office, keeping it there as a reference should he need it, and within a fortnight has forgotten all about the workshop. A pity, really, there was some good stuff in it...

put new learning into practice. Support can also be demonstrated in other ways by peers' willingness to stand in while colleagues are involved in training. As we saw, peer support can also be forthcoming from fellow attendees from the network that often builds up around a programme. All co-participants, with wide experience from their current and previous jobs, can bring to bear on problems discussed a wealth of expertise from their knowledge of similar situations.

Of course not all peers support each other. In some work environments individualism is the order of the day and it's not at all unusual for peers to be quite indifferent to the efforts of others to try out new things. They may even demonstrate a degree of hostility where threats to the status quo in terms of status or influence might be perceived.

## Support From the Organization

As described earlier, the presence of organization support – the extent to which trainees are provided with or obtain resources and opportunities on-the-job that enable them to use the skills taught in training – also contributes to the creation of a climate for transfer. This is reflected in the literature, as all of the studies cited above have made reference to specific support from the organization as a component of climate (particularly Clarke 2002; Awoniyi et al. 2002). Those organizational support elements regularly highlighted have included issues around resources and workloads; urgency and deadlines; and autonomy and creativity.

### RESOURCES AND WORKLOADS

High on the list of constraints to effective application is the lack of spare capacity in human resources to allow time for practice and development of new skills. This is seen for example in the case of managers returning to work from a management development programme, and then struggling to engage in 'management' rather than 'operational' activity. Numbers are often already tight, and releasing staff for appropriate training may be sometimes impossible due to the risk of leaving the department exposed at the front line, or indeed even contravene particular health or safety practices. This can have an effect on morale, which in turn can affect absenteeism, generating a vicious circle.

Lack of availability of other resources also inhibits learning transfer. In some cases, this may be a lack of technical resources such as IT tools and systems, which if available would free up staff to engage in work that makes a better contribution to their department or work unit. This of course may be due to financial constraints, which are an ongoing challenge to departments and organizations everywhere. Convincing those who have control over such resources, and who may not be able to see the benefits of investment in people development will always be a battle.

---

### BOX 4.2: THE IMPORTANCE OF THE WORK ENVIRONMENT

The following observations are taken from an evaluation report around a range of different training and development programmes delivered for a medium-sized public service organization. Data were gathered from two sources – focus groups drawn from participants who had attended at least one of the programmes in the previous year's portfolio, and responses to a questionnaire designed by the author, the Learning Transfer Evaluation (LTE). Within the focus groups, participants reported a wide range of organizational factors that helped or hindered them in applying learning from the courses they attended. These factors related to manager, peer and organizational support as well as the climate for change within their work environments. In general they saw it as helpful if:

- their boss was convinced of the value of the training they (the participants) attended;
- they were given the opportunity for 'refresher' sessions, particularly in the case of practical skills;
- they were able to get access to one-to-one support afterwards, particularly for practical skills;
- they could participate in a discussion forum, perhaps delivered via the organization's intranet;
- they had a degree of autonomy in their jobs

Equally, it was seen as unhelpful if:

- the training they attended wasn't linked to organizational needs or priorities;
- the training they attended wasn't directly linked to their own training needs;
- managers higher up in the organization didn't support training;
- their own manager didn't get involved pre- or post-training;
- they didn't use the new skill they acquired soon and regularly;
- others around them didn't 'buy in'.

Data from the LTE supported opinions coming from the focus groups. Amongst other factors, the LTE measures participant perceptions of *manager support and coaching, peer support* and *climate for transfer,* the main workplace influences on learning transfer, with *manager support and coaching* being the most crucial. On all three dimensions, LTE respondents rated them (on a scale of 1-5) on average 3.09, 3.16 and 3.23 respectively. However, the spread of scores was of greater interest than the average scores. For *manager support and coaching,* for instance, scores ranged from 1.00 to 4.67. This indicated a wide disparity in the levels of support offered to participants from their respective bosses. A similar picture emerged regarding *climate for transfer*, a factor influenced by the level of *manager support and coaching*. The scores for *peer support,* while nowhere near as variable, pointed to a situation in which, while the level of support for training from these quarters was not a particular hindrance, neither was it particularly strong.

As described in the model outlined in Chapter 1, the combined effect of these three factors works on the participant's *personal ability to transfer* (the amount of time and mental space they can make to apply their learning). Not surprisingly, this figure came in somewhere in the middle (average score 3.18) with a relatively small amount of variation. Once again, this suggests that participants returning from interventions in that organization would have something of a challenge on their hands to apply what they learned. Recommendations to the organization which were subsequently implemented included the initiation of individual pre-and post-course meetings between participants and their boss (to raise the level of *manager support and coaching*) and the establishment of a series of follow-up problem-solving sessions within departmental units (to improve the *climate for transfer*).

## URGENCY AND DEADLINES

The nature of many work environments is that people have an awful lot to do and very little time to do it. This situation is usually related to a greater or lesser extent to the constraints outlined above. Often as a result of these constraints, a culture of short-term goals and short-term priorities can evolve, making it even more difficult to pay attention to longer-term, less urgent priorities. This can have important implications for the level of support provided both before and after formal training interventions. In these environments, training and development is more likely to be seen as something for which trainers are solely responsible. Yet the evidence consistently shows that investment in organizational support pays dividends. Some organizations have processes whereby those participating on programmes perhaps go through a selection process, discussing potential outcomes with their boss or someone in the learning and development department, thus better integrating the individual's learning needs with those of the organization. Stronger links between the content of the programme and its application to their own work situation, through better identification of their job priorities and their developmental needs are the result. Post-programme, asking participants to make presentations about salient parts of the programme to colleagues (perhaps even making it a condition of attendance) has been seen to help generalize learning.

## AUTONOMY AND CREATIVITY

Another barrier to transferring learning appears to arise from structural issues within the organization itself. It seems that the latitude people have to make changes in their behaviour back at work depends to some extent on the degree to which autonomy and initiative are encouraged and rewarded. People in some organizations and work units, typically newer, smaller and less formal ones, have more freedom to make the changes they see as appropriate. They are more likely to describe their organization as having a lack of bureaucracy, a non-hierarchical 'climate' within the work unit, and a way of working that supports development and the sharing of learning. On the other hand, in (perhaps) larger, older organizations the general level of bureaucracy can have an effect on the ability to transfer through interfering with opportunities to use learning. People in these situations are more likely to report inordinate amounts of time to get things done, for example, approval to attend a developmental seminar or visit another organization. These difficulties can be exacerbated where there is a sensitive industrial relations climate, and where some training outcomes may be difficult to apply due to changes in roles or duties.

## Support From Your Manager

As has already been seen in the previous section, supportive management and supervisory behaviours contribute to a positive organizational climate for transfer. They will be discussed more specifically here. The work of many people since the 1950s has emphasized the importance of support from the immediate boss of participants on training and development programmes. Later work (Seyler et al. 1998; Lim and Johnsson 2002; Gumuseli and Ergin 2002), conducted in a variety of organizational settings has reinforced the results of earlier work – that the level of manager or supervisory support can significantly influence learning transfer.

Two very clear times at which manager support can manifest itself are immediately before and immediately after the participant's attendance at a training programme. As well as other forms of support, having a pre-programme discussion with an intending participant and following up afterwards have been shown in particular to improve transfer. Studies by Brinkerhoff and Montesino (1995) and Gregoire, Propp and Poertner (1998) looked at specific actions taken by managers before and after training interventions. The kind of supports they reviewed included setting expectations for learning and usage

---

**BOX 4.3: THE SUPPORTIVE MANAGER**

Ana is a recently-appointed Head of Unit in a policy unit within a pan-European development agency. She has found herself with a challenging job, responsible for the output and career development of some 15 staff. Her unit comprises a mixture of newer and longer-serving staff, with corresponding levels of enthusiasm for their work. Ana recently attended an 8-day management development programme aimed at helping her meet those challenges. The programme included inputs on the role of the manager, setting objectives and managing performance, as well as team-working and managing change. Following the programme, her motivation to transfer what she has learned is high, given that what she focused on during the programme is exactly what she requires help in. Her action plan is specifically around getting to grips with some of the 'problem people' in her unit.

She's lucky in one respect. Her director Maria understands the importance of effective people management, and was the person who suggested Ana's participation in the programme in the first place. They had an in-depth discussion about it, and agreed suitable outcomes and priorities. Indeed Ana has had many discussions of this nature with Maria since she joined the unit and has received some quite useful guidance and feedback along the way.

So, not surprisingly, just 2 days after her return from the programme, Maria is looking to meet with her to see how the programme went, and what she has learned that might be useful. They discuss some of the highlights and begin to look at Ana's action plan. Maria asks Ana about how she intends to proceed. Ana outlines her thoughts, focusing on the first conversation she's going to have with Eric, one of the 'problem people' identified. Maria listens, asking some well-placed questions of clarification, while resisting the urge to advise Ana directly. Ana suggests that one option she'd like to consider is to move Eric to a role within the section which she believes would be more suited to his talents. A few more questions from Maria satisfy her as to Ana's motives and she agrees to proceed. She asks Ana if she would like her to attend the meeting, and accepts Ana's decision that she can handle it herself. They agree a meeting to follow up on the session with Eric and will decide where to go from there.

---

of learning on-the-job, help in deciding what training is needed, help with the trainee's caseload to attend training and encouragement to try out new skills.

## What Manager Support Looks Like

Experience with organizational environments and evaluation of learning interventions consistently indicates that the level of manager support for participants returning from those interventions can vary considerably within and across organizations, from unsupportive through neutral to very supportive. Piecing together responses from a recently undertaken study (Kirwan 2005), a composite picture of what a supportive manager looks like in practice is presented and discussed below.

## SUPPORTIVE MANAGERS EMPOWER OTHERS

One of the most significant ways in which managers can facilitate transfer is through their encouragement and empowerment of their staff, generating a belief in their (the staff member's) own ability. Critical in this regard is a 'hands off' type of approach that seems to be appreciated by so many staff. They value the support that is available, yet they are happy to be allowed to 'get on with it'. This is certainly indicative of a more empowering style of management, and is important from the point of view of staff maintaining confidence in their own ability to do the job. The importance of generating and maintaining this confidence (self-efficacy) will be discussed further in Chapter 5. In the meantime, how this is done is clear enough to see from the evidence. Managers who allow their staff to perform as they think appropriate send a clear message concerning confidence in their staff's ability to do the job. Yet at the same time, being available for support ensures that should the need arise, advice can be sought. The autonomy experienced by staff allows them the freedom to take courses of action and make their own decisions, with consequent reported effects for their self-efficacy. This type of support is central to the role of the manager as a coach. We saw in Chapter 3 the value to be gained from using a coach, and its importance as a learning transfer tool. The behaviours of managers as coaches are just the same. More supportive managers regularly ask questions, although they're not slow to give advice when they feel it's needed. They also spend time to help the person being coached to decide the area(s) on which the coaching will be focused; they work with the person to get a clear sense of what outcomes are desired and where the person 'is' at the moment; and they work with the person to agree a series of steps to close the gap. They demonstrate these behaviours in particular before staff attend learning events, and continue it on their return.

## SUPPORTIVE MANAGERS DELEGATE EFFECTIVELY

An important component of the 'hands off' style discussed above is of course delegation. Supportive managers are usually good at delegation, and are not afraid to allow their staff to 'get on with the job'. When considered as a development process, effective delegation can be a very powerful method of learning, and the evidence for this is hard to argue against. Effective delegation requires the provision of clarity around the goal to be achieved, and the monitoring of progress through feedback and coaching. Not surprisingly, all of these activities are also generally regarded as supportive of learning transfer.

## SUPPORTIVE MANAGERS LISTEN AND SHOW EMPATHY

Supportive managers who facilitate learning transfer also tend to listen better than those who don't. While this is seen as part and parcel of a manager's job in many organizations, it's a skill that should not be taken for granted. Active listening is an important element in demonstrating empathy. Empathy is about understanding issues from another's point of view, and is a skill (along with the skill of active listening) in short supply in many work environments. One of the effects of

---

### BOX 4.4: THE NON-SUPPORTIVE MANAGER

Sean is the head of a newly formed unit within a long established insurance company. The staff, totalling 12 in all, for which Sean is responsible, come mostly from sales backgrounds. One of the reasons Sean was asked to take the job was because of a need to, in his director's words, 'remotivate the team' and come up with some innovative ideas for transforming the culture from a low risk one – concentrating on established customers with established products – to a more dynamic one in which new business opportunities involving the company's more innovative products are pursued with enthusiasm.

It's not easy. Although Sean is not new to the business of people management, managing this team can be a bit of a struggle. The structure of the company, which is a bit old-fashioned and somewhat hierarchical means that more power than perhaps is prudent is vested in those higher up the ladder, despite their degree of remove from what's happening on the ground. At Sean's interview for the job it was recommended that he undertake a short programme entitled *How to manage your sales staff.* The objective of this programme is primarily to understand the importance of creating conditions where staff will be motivated to sell, no mean feat in itself. He has just finished the programme, and has picked up a number of things he'd like to try out.

His first thought on his return is to have a chat with is boss, Mark. However, Mark is a hard man to pin down. They never did get to talk before he went on the programme, and indeed Sean is not too sure Mark really knows what the programme was about. Finally, after several attempts, he manages to arrange a date and time in Mark's diary, 15 minutes before lunch on Tuesday next. He starts to outline to Mark the issues he'd like to bring up at the meeting, but is told that it will all keep until Tuesday. Late on Monday afternoon he gets a call to rearrange the meeting to the same time on Thursday.

On Thursday, he arrives with his thoughts in order. Mark spends the first 5 minutes outlining his own plans for Sean's department, and once again it's only through the persistence his selling skills training taught him that he manages to get Mark to concentrate on the original agenda. High on that agenda is a proposal to change the bonus system from an individual system to a group system, as Sean sees much greater potential in collaboration than in competition between his sales team members. They talk about it (or rather Sean does) before Mark gives his verdict. It's not going to happen, as, in his words, 'the only way to motivate sales people is to get them competing against each other – you get much better performance that way'. He won't discuss or explain his thinking to Sean, arguing that 'in my position you have to make decisions, and that's what I'm doing now'. Sean wonders why he bothered going on the training programme in the first place...

demonstrating empathy is that it can allow issues that may be lurking beneath the surface of a problem to be raised, making them visible and therefore easier to deal with. From a learning point of view this is particularly important, as it facilitates a greater understanding of learner difficulties and barriers to transfer.

## SUPPORTIVE MANAGERS GENERATE A SUPPORTIVE CLIMATE

Empathy and its constituent parts, good listening and questioning skills, are important contributors in creating a climate of openness, a regularly cited characteristic attributed to supportive managers (Bennett, Lehman and Forst 1999). It is particularly important as a transfer-facilitating behaviour in the context of communicating with staff. Supportive managers keep their staff up-to-date with what's going on in the department and provide clarity when and where they can. Supportive managers also demonstrate an open style of management with their staff, particularly in terms of more involvement in meetings, projects and task groups. In a broader sense, supportive managers hold positive attitudes about the benefits of education and development, as well the need to share them. Finally, creating a climate of openness is also about being open to new ways of doing things, and is reinforced by the encouragement of autonomy, initiative and creativity, factors which we saw are important in organizational climates for transfer.

## SUPPORTIVE MANAGERS EXERT A WIDER INFLUENCE

Managers who are considered most supportive seem to take a broader, more strategic view of their area of responsibility and its people. In addition, they are always ready to look at possibilities and problems in an analytic, constructive way, and give the benefit of their experience (often by being 'devil's advocate') when giving advice or making recommendations. Finally, another important way in which managers are seen as supportive is through their influence with the wider organization, perhaps acting as informal mentors.

## MANAGER SUPPORT IN CONTEXT

It would appear from the picture described above that the behaviours that characterize manager support for transfer are essentially the more 'people-oriented' behaviours found in the management style frameworks of theorists such as Hersey and Blanchard (1982) or Tannenbaum and Schmidt (1973). For example, Hersey and Blanchard's framework displays a style continuum ranging from authoritative to delegative (telling-selling-participating-delegating). Similarly, Tannenbaum and Schmidt's continuum is anchored by autocratic at one end and democratic at the other. Perhaps it is that people who work for supportive managers are likely to feel more confident that learning from interventions they attend is less likely to be wasted. Thus it would appear that at least one important consequence of being a 'people-oriented' manager is that it improves the likelihood of learning being transferred for the staff of that manager.

Finally, a summary of the type of supports offered by peers, managers and the organization is provided in Table 4.3.

## In Practice

In some cases, as we have seen, the work environment can be a rich source of support for individuals in their efforts to make practical sense of what they have learned when they get back to work. In others, it can be a difficult place to navigate through, requiring a high degree of motivation and tenacity to turn good intentions into reality. Therefore, in order to maximize the positive effects of the supports and minimize the negative effects of the barriers, some of the following learning transfer strategies should be adopted where appropriate.

## SET UP BUDDY SYSTEMS

A technique that many participants have found beneficial following attendance at a programme is to work with another individual who has attended the same programme. This activity is usually linked to each participant's action plan. For example, they can agree to be available to each other as a resource to test, question or provide advice. Another important role they can play is that of the other's conscience, providing timely reminders regarding steps in the action

Table 4.3     Types of manager, peer and organizational support

| Manager support | Peer support | Organization support |
|---|---|---|
| Enthusiasm for change | Enthusiasm for change | Provision of financial support |
| Openness to new ideas | Willingness to try out new ideas | for learning efforts |
| Showing empathy | Listening | Involvement of local |
| Listening | Giving supportive feedback | management in the learning |
| Discussing strengths and | Giving constructive criticism | process |
| weaknesses | Giving a different perspective | Provision of coaching (external) |
| Giving constructive criticism | 'Plugging the gaps' | Development of managers as |
| Giving supportive feedback | Availability of network | coaches (internal) |
| Generating participant's belief | Showing tolerance and | Arrangement of alumni sessions |
| in their own ability | understanding | Establishment of communities |
| Empowering | | of practice |
| Delegating | | |
| Playing 'devil's advocate' | | |
| Being available | | |
| Communicating | | |
| Using influence with others | | |

plan that were agreed at the programme. The benefits of using co-attendees on a programme for support have already been discussed in Chapter 3.

## GET A 'CRITICAL MASS' ON THE SAME PROGRAMME

Although it can be logistically difficult in many instances, there can be very positive implications for transfer by having a number of people from the same department or work unit attend the same programme. Benefits include the reinforcement of important ideas or attitudes and mutual support for their implementation. In these situations the programme can become a framework within which real world issues can be dealt with, using common approaches and even a common language. Going a step further, some organizations develop programmes built around intact teams or work units, where the entire team attends the same programme at the same time. In approach, this resembles action learning, and as such has positive implications for learning transfer.

## INCLUDE GUIDANCE ON PRE- AND POST-TRAINING DISCUSSIONS WITH THE JOINING INSTRUCTIONS

Although this can also be classed as a management support issue, organizations can benefit at the broader level from introducing a degree of formalization into the process. While the most important element in the process is the dialogue that takes place between the manager and the person attending the training, the collective outputs from these discussions could provide a wealth of useful information for the person providing the training on the one hand, and function as an indicator of organizational training needs on the other. To facilitate the process, a template to guide the discussions could be included with the joining instructions.

## REFUND FEES/EXPENSES/AWARDS

One practical way in which organizations can provide at least some incentive for their staff to engage in self-development is through contributing towards the activity, either in terms of sponsorship for particular programmes or courses of study, or by way of awards (especially financial) for undertaking and successfully getting through them. While other factors, particularly those relating to generating the motivation to learn need to be in place, the prospect of the fees being refunded, or better still a cash award on completion may remove the last barriers to taking them on.

## ENCOURAGE PRESENTATIONS AND KNOWLEDGE SHARING SESSIONS

Some organizations already have this process in place, and it can be a very useful practice to initiate. A typical arrangement is that, in return for an individual being allowed to attend a particular training programme or conference, they are required on their return to present to their colleagues the highlights, key learning points and potential applications of the learning. In this way, knowledge is transferred throughout the unit. As well as benefitting the unit, it also provides a focus for the individual who attended the programme, in that it forces them to consider what learning was valuable and how it might be applied back at work.

## PROMOTE ALUMNI SESSIONS

Opportunities to revisit prior learning, develop new learning and catch up with colleagues or others who have attended a similar event also help bring learning from the back of a participant's mind to the front of it. While the focus should be primarily on consolidating learning, such sessions can also provide an opportunity to explore what issues and challenges are to be faced in the future, and begin building a response.

## ESTABLISH COMMUNITIES OF PRACTICE

In the context of learning transfer, communities of practice (Lave and Wenger 1991) are essentially groups (either naturally occurring or created for a specific purpose) that come together to share their expertise to solve problems and provide mutual support. In that respect, they have many of the characteristics of action learning groups. Setting up these 'user groups' provides a forum for exchange of ideas and identification of further needs. Communities of practice can exist for people managers, for project managers, for sales people, for users of specific IT applications, for personality test users, indeed almost any group of individuals that share common learning needs.

## INVOLVE MANAGERS BEFORE TRAINING

Every participant needs to know what they will gain from their investment of time and energy in attending a programme. Given the multitude of demands on their time, the perceived benefits need to be made very clear. As such, a vital element in the overall process is a pre-programme meeting with their immediate boss. This meeting should be used to identify reasons for attending the programme, the main areas for development, expectations and possible applications of learning and how the programme might be used to address these. It is at this stage that a learning contract between the two can be agreed, which specifies the commitment and support that will be required from both parties. The meeting can also be used to discuss outputs from any pre-programme work, if appropriate.

## INVOLVE MANAGERS AFTER TRAINING

This is crucial in terms of 'closing the loop' begun with the pre-programme meeting. Plans for implementation of the participant's action plan should be discussed, and barriers and supports to implementation identified. It's an essential element in helping to generalize and maintain new knowledge and learned skills in the workplace. In this regard, managers who are skilled in coaching are in a position to be of most help.

## DEVELOP MANAGERS AS COACHES

The role of the manager as coach is one which has perhaps been seriously underestimated in the past. All the evidence seen here so far supports the idea that for effective learning transfer to take place, managers of training participants need to demonstrate the skills of listening, delegation, feedback (and others) in order to create the conditions where their staff can learn and develop. Learning and development is central to effective performance, and in turn effective performance is central to motivation and satisfaction. For this reason, developing the coaching skills of managers is a very sound investment. Managers as coaches fulfil many of the tasks identified in Chapter 3 and in this one, seen as critical in facilitating transfer.

---

**BOX 4.5: THE CASE FOR MANAGERS AS COACHES**

Two separate studies, conducted recently in similar organizations (medium-sized public sector agencies) revealed in passing a strong case for encouraging line managers to engage in more coaching-type behaviours to support the learning and development of their staff. One of the studies was an evaluation of one agency's training and development activity in the previous year. The other was an investigation, carried out immediately after delivery of the pilot of a team leader development programme, of workplace factors likely to affect learning transfer from the programme. Between the two studies some 54 responses were analyzed.

In short, it was clearly obvious in the case of both organizations that the line managers concerned (in most instances highly qualified technical people) played little or no active part in the learning process for their staff. Only three had any sort of pre-programme discussion with their staff, and none followed up afterwards. As a consequence of this lack of engagement by those managers, the following (negative) outcomes were reported.

- Most of the respondents had attended at least one workshop, programme or conference that was of little relevance to their job. For example, three of the 24 respondents who attended the team leader development programme did not in fact manage any staff.
- Nine respondents made specific reference to difficulties encountered in trying out new ideas back at work. These ideas included a new format for team meetings, a more efficient rostering system and a small change to a staff incentive scheme. In each case, the respondents cited resistance from their boss as the major barrier.
- Apart from task-related feedback, only four respondents overall reported getting useful (whether positive or negative) developmental feedback from their line manager in the previous year.

Overall, the level of motivation reported by respondents in the two studies was not at all high. For those who had some enthusiasm for making changes back at work, they felt somewhat isolated. For the others, they had essentially given up trying to do so.

## Summary

There is plenty of evidence in the literature concerning the significance of work environment factors in either inhibiting or facilitating transfer of learning from training programmes. Qualitative studies have identified a range of factors such as workload and other pressures, resource issues, and the presence or absence of support from peers, supervisors and the organization. Particular attention has been focused on the idea of a climate for transfer, a set of interacting workplace factors that facilitate or inhibit application of skills and knowledge learned in training back on-the-job.

Within this climate, the role of manager support has been emphasized, taking the form of specific pre- and post-training support, on-the-job coaching and providing opportunities for the trainee to use learning. In summary, what the studies tend to agree on is the role this combination and interaction of factors plays in creating conditions that help either trainees' ability to transfer, their motivation to transfer or both.

## References

Awoniyi, E.A., Griego, O.V. and Morgan, G.A. (2002). Person-environment fit and transfer of training. *International Journal of Training and Development*, 6(1), 25–35.

Baumgartel, H. and Jeanpierre, F. (1972). Applying new knowledge in the back-home setting: A study of Indian managers' adoptive efforts. *Journal of Applied Behavioural Science*, 8, 674–94.

Bennett, J.B., Lehman, W.E.K. and Forst, J.K. (1999). Change, transfer climate and customer orientation: A contextual model and analysis of change-driven training. *Group and Organization Management*, 24, 188–216.

Brinkerhoff, R.O. and Montesino, M.U. (1995). Partnerships for training transfer: Lessons from a corporate study. *Human Resource Development Quarterly*, 6, 263–74.

Clarke, N. (2002). Job/work environment factors influencing training transfer within a human service agency: Some indicative support for Baldwin and Ford's transfer climate construct. *International Journal of Training and Development*, 6(3), 146–62.

Gregoire, T.K., Propp, J. and Poertner, J. (1998). The supervisor's role in the transfer of training. *Administration in Social Work*, 22(1), 1–18.

Gumuseli, A.I. and Ergin, B. (2002). The manager's role in enhancing the transfer of training: A Turkish case study. *International Journal of Training and Development*, 6(2), 80–97.

Hersey, P. and Blanchard, K.L. (1982). *Management of organizational behavior: Utilizing human resources. 4th ed.* Englewood Cliffs, NJ; Prentice-Hall.

Huczynski, A.A. (1977). Organisational climates and the transfer of learning. *BACIE Journal*, 31(6), 98–9.

Huczynski, A.A. and Lewis, J.W. (1980). An empirical study into the learning transfer process in management training. *Journal of Management Studies*, 17, 227–40.

Kirwan, C. (2005). *Transfer of learning: Understanding the process and test of a model.* Unpublished doctoral thesis. Henley Management College/Brunel University.

Lave, J. and Wenger, E. (1991). *Situated learning: Legitimate peripheral participation.* New York, NY: Cambridge University Press.

Lim, D.H. and Johnson, S.D. (2002). Trainees' perceptions of factors that influence learning transfer. *International Journal of Training and Development,* 6(1), 36–48.

Noe, R.A. (1986). Trainees' attributes and attitudes: Neglected influences on training effectiveness. *Academy of Management Review,* 11, 736–49.

Rouiller, J.Z. and Goldstein, I.L. (1993). The relationship between organizational transfer climate and positive transfer of training. *Human Resource Development Quarterly,* 4, 377–90.

Seyler, D.L., Holton, E.F., III. Bates, R.A., Burnett, M.F. and Carvalho, M.A. (1998). Factors affecting motivation to transfer training. *International Journal of Training and Development,* 2(1), 2–16.

Smith, P.A. and O'Neil, J. (2003a). A review of action learning literature 1994–2000: Part 2 – signposts into the literature. *Journal of Workplace Learning,* 15(4), 154–66.

Smith, P.A. and O'Neil, J. (2003b). A review of action learning literature 1994–2000: Part 1 – bibliography and comments. *Journal of Workplace Learning,* 15(2), 63–9.

Tannenbaum, R. and Schmidt, W.H. (1973). How to choose a leadership pattern. *Harvard Business Review,* 51, 166–68.

Tracey, J.B., Tannenbaum, S.I. and Kavanagh, M.J. (1995). Applying trained skills on the job: The importance of the work environment. *Journal of Applied Psychology,* 80, 239–52.

Yorks, L., O'Neil, J., Marsick, V.J., Lamm, S., Kolodny, R. and Nilson, G. (1998). Transfer of learning from an action-reflection-learning program. *Performance Improvement Quarterly,* 11(1), 59–73.

# 5

# It's up to You: Making it Happen

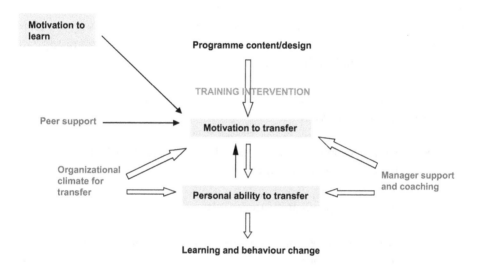

## Introduction

If you're putting together a training or development programme, ensuring that participants will be motivated to learn from it and subsequently motivated to transfer that learning is a major challenge. A further challenge in turning motivation to learn and to transfer into actual learning transfer is finding the time and mental space to do so. It's this attribute we call personal ability to transfer. All these factors will be discussed in this chapter.

Not surprisingly, the sources of motivation can be many. We saw in Chapter 2 that training design factors can have a significant influence on motivation to learn and to transfer. In Chapter 3, the emphasis was on activities that help to bridge the gap between the classroom and the workplace. Then, in Chapter 4, a number of organizational conditions that affect motivation were discussed, namely peer support, manager support and organization support.

However, research by this author (Kirwan 2005a) supports the consensus evident in the literature that motivational factors are more strongly related to personal attributes than to other factors. So, if this is the case, how can they be influenced? In truth, there will be many occasions where they cannot, but nevertheless they are factors worth knowing about. They are particularly relevant if you want to understand, in your role as a manager for example, what might be helping or hindering one of your staff in translating learned knowledge or skill back to work. Or you may be a learning and development manager selecting candidates for a particular high profile or pilot programme, and want to improve the chances of transfer. Finally, if you are operating in the role of a coach, then an understanding of a particular individual's approach to learning and its application can help both of you identify the most appropriate course of action to make it happen.

From what is in the research literature, those most likely to learn (and use that learning) are those who:

- have a clear expectation of what they want to 'get out of' any learning intervention they attend;

- have positive job and career attitudes;

- attribute success or failure to their own efforts (have an internal locus of control);

- are concerned with mastering a skill rather than just performing better than others (have a mastery orientation);

- have a strong belief in their ability to learn from the intervention and use it (have high self-efficacy).

Each of these factors will be explained and discussed in turn. The primary influences on motivation are shown in Figure 5.1 (thick arrows indicate strong relationships while thinner arrows suggest a weaker relationship).

As can be seen in the model, many of the relevant personal attributes exert their effect on individuals' motivation to learn, and through it, their motivation to transfer. Some attributes, such as self-efficacy for example, are more strongly felt on motivation to transfer. However, they will all be discussed in the context of motivation.

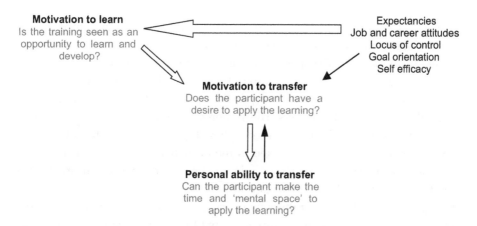

**Figure 5.1    Influences on motivation to transfer learning**

## The Importance of Motivation

We often hear people say things like 'I feel really de-motivated today' or 'I really must motivate myself to take more exercise'. What do people mean when they say that? Definitions of motivation abound but probably the best way to think about motivation is in terms of what makes people want to put in extra effort, to really give of their best in the interests of achieving something.

As such it is a hugely important element in performance at work. Having all the right skills for the job is of course also critical, but it's only the starting point. The 'right people' will not remain so if opportunities for them to be motivated do not exist in the context of their work, or if their performance is badly managed. Much of this motivation will come from what they learn and how they use it to improve their performance. Therefore, understanding what motivates people, and creating conditions at work that make the best use of these motivators, is one of the most important competencies that managers can develop. For this reason, motivation will first be discussed in a general context, and then more specifically in the context of learning and learning transfer.

### MOTIVATION AND EFFORT

When individuals start considering what motivates them at work, they usually begin with the things that they feel good about doing, the rewards of the job. Different people, at different times, will look for different rewards, such as recognition, being part of a successful team, a good salary, the opportunity to achieve something of importance or helping others. They will put in effort to achieve these things. These differences are at the heart of the cognitive approach to behaviour, which we saw in Chapter 1 focuses on what's going on inside the learner's head. On top of that, people will usually only put in effort to achieve these rewards if they have an expectation that the effort will pay off in some way. An example might be taking on extra work in the belief that it will lead to promotion or gain the approval of their peers. This notion is central to the expectancy theory of motivation (Vroom 1964). Thirdly, people will be less inclined to put in effort if they think too much is being asked of them, such as goals they can't achieve or just too much work. Similarly, people will be less inclined to put in effort if they don't see any challenge in what they're doing, for example a boring job, or a lack of direction. In both of these cases, people see a large gap between what they think they can do (their ability) and what they feel is being asked of them (the demands). Finally, people will be less motivated to put in effort if they feel they are not being treated fairly relative to others. This perception can arise either because they feel other people aren't putting in as much effort as they are, or that others' rewards are greater for the amount of effort they do put in. This aspect of motivation is described by equity theory (Adams 1963).

One theme that runs through the above observations is that ultimately, people are motivated to put in effort to achieve things that make them feel good about themselves directly (through recognition of a job well done, or successfully overcoming a challenge, for instance) or indirectly (through a bonus or a larger company car). That is why sometimes people don't even put any effort into trying to overcome particular challenges if they think that challenge will be too great – they know they won't succeed and trying and failing will not make them feel good about themselves. These ideas are based on work by Bandura (1986) and others on the subject of self-efficacy, a central element in motivation.

## MOTIVATION AND SATISFACTION

If one looks back at the list of motivators, it's quite likely that the things on that list are related to the job itself, such as successfully meeting a deadline, or having a customer write a nice 'thank you' letter. This is not unusual. Most people regard these factors (*intrinsic* factors) as more important than many others, such as a good salary, a nice office, and so on (*extrinsic* factors). What's interesting about extrinsic factors is that they tend to be of less significance when intrinsic factors are having a motivating effect, and of more significance when they're not, or if extrinsic factors themselves are not positive (Herzberg 1968). For example, staff will not start working harder every time they get a salary increase, but if they feel their salary is not good (compared with others, perhaps) it can cause demotivation.

## What the Literature Says

As indicated earlier, the literature relating to motivation and learning transfer has focused on some key areas, which will now be discussed.

### EXPECTANCIES

One of the first questions participants are likely to ask themselves before embarking on a training or development programme is how useful the programme is likely to be to them in their work, and whether their efforts to attend and learn from it will 'pay off'. A number of studies have looked at this (Huczynski and Lewis 1980; Hicks and Klimowski 1987; Baldwin, Magjuka and Loher 1991; Clark, Dobbins and Ladd 1993; Cheng 2000) and have linked effort/ performance expectancies (the belief that effort expended in training will result in learning), and performance/outcome expectancies (the belief that learning will lead to successful performance on-the-job) to motivation to learn. These studies have demonstrated that trainees' perception regarding whether they have a choice to attend or not attend a training programme can strongly influence their motivation to learn and subsequently their learning on the programme. In a similar way, trainees' participation in the choice of training content can also affect their motivation to learn (provided they are ultimately given the training of their choice). It seems that offering a choice plays a very important part in increasing feelings of mastery and self-determination, which in turn increase motivation.

Knowing what to expect from a programme does not necessarily mean knowing the content in detail before the programme begins. According to the research evidence, those more motivated to learn, particularly on broader development programmes as opposed to more specific training programmes, are those that see the programme as an opportunity to learn something new and useful (whatever that might be), and who tend therefore to approach it in an open frame of mind.

### HOW IT WORKS

Vroom's (1964) theory of motivation provides a suitable explanatory framework. His model comprises three elements. The first is *expectancy* – the belief that putting in a certain level of effort will result in a certain level of performance (first level outcomes). The second is *instrumentality* – that attaining that level of performance will result in certain desired outcomes (second level outcomes). The third is the *valence* – the individual's preference for a particular second level outcome. Put in plain English, it looks like:

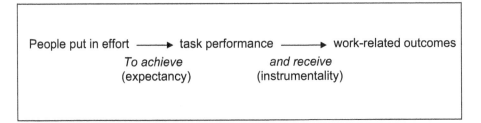

**Figure 5.2    Performance expectancies**

An example should help with clarification. Suppose an ambitious young client relationship manager is asked to take part in a new development programme, which will result in a sizeable investment of their time. Although there is no extra salary involved, they understand that participation on this programme will raise their profile amongst more senior managers, and make promotion (something they want) more likely. In Vroom's terms, the prospect of promotion has a high *valence* for them. If promotion is something they are not particularly interested in, then the proposition has a low valence. Also in this case, they have an *expectancy* that if they work hard on the programme, they will perform well on it and make a good impression. If they believe that good performance will result in the promotion they seek, then the relationship between the first- and second-level outcomes has high *instrumentality*. If of course they don't believe that good performance on the programme will result in the promotion they want, then the relationship has low instrumentality, and their motivation to participate on the programme will be lower.

There is another reason that participants may want to attend a programme, quite apart from the content of the programme. More and more, people who work in smaller organizations (as well as those who work in larger, spread-out organizations) value the opportunity to get to know a network of others in similar situations. They use this opportunity to exchange notes and 'benchmark' themselves with individuals in similar situations and with similar issues. Some programme design elements that can facilitate such interaction were discussed in Chapter 2. Outcomes from such interaction can be quite rewarding, and even if people don't find solutions to their work problems, at the very least they may be able to reassure themselves that 'they are not alone'. This is a legitimate outcome which in turn has an effect on their confidence to tackle those problems. Learner confidence is discussed later.

## JOB AND CAREER ATTITUDES

It should come as no surprise to hear that participants who have more positive attitudes to their jobs tend to be more motivated to learn and transfer their learning more successfully. Evidence for this comes from a number of sources (Noe and Schmitt 1986; Tannenbaum et al. 1991; Tesluk et al. 1995; Facteau et al. 1995). Both high job involvement (the extent to which people identify with work or the importance of work for their self-image) and high organizational commitment (the extent to which they identify with and are involved in a particular organization) have been found to be related to motivation to learn and to transfer of skills learned to the job. In some of these studies, a negative correlation between organizational cynicism and generalization has also been demonstrated.

## HOW IT WORKS

People are chosen to attend training courses for a number of reasons. One of the reasons they can be chosen is that their managers may see development potential in them. In such cases, nomination for a programme, particularly if it is one with a high profile, for example at a major business school, can be seen as a reward, or at least as some recognition of commitment. Thus how the programme opportunity is presented to individuals can be important. We'll see more of this when we talk about self-efficacy shortly.

## LOCUS OF CONTROL

Another personality dimension that has received some attention in the transfer literature is that of locus of control (Kelly 1955). It refers to the perceived source of control over one's behaviour. People with an internal locus of control tend to attribute success or failure to their own efforts, whilst those with an external locus of control see success or failure as more to do with outside forces. Although not much work has been done in this area recently, some early studies (Baumgartel and Jeanpierre 1972; Baumgartel, Reynolds and Pathan 1984) with American and with Indian managers found significant relationships between locus of control and efforts to apply knowledge. They have supported the view that those with an internal locus of control will make a greater effort to apply the training, seeing success in training as being something under their own control.

## HOW IT WORKS

The notion of attribution (Heider 1958) is significant in terms of motivation. In general terms, attributing success to internal causes helps improve self-efficacy, while attributing failure to external causes helps maintain it. For example, supposing a young car sales executive has come away from a sales development programme with a challenging goal to be achieved – to improve their skill in negotiating a better price for the sale. They begin to practise on their first, smaller deal, and as would be expected, don't get everything right the first time. They may react in a number of ways. For instance, they might console themself with the fact that the particular car they were trying to sell was a heap of junk anyway ('not even Larry the showroom legend could have sold it'). In this case, they are *attributing* failure to sell the car to external causes. This enables them to maintain their self-efficacy, that is, their belief that they can actually negotiate and sell cars. In the same way, if they had managed to be very successful the first time out, it would help their motivation to go on and perform even better if they were to attribute the success to their own efforts ('I listened to what I was being taught and really worked hard at it'). Conversely, people who attribute failure to internal causes, for example, ('I'm not really any good at this') or success to external causes ('I was lucky the right questions came up on the paper') do not improve their self-efficacy and consequently may make it harder to motivate themselves for the next challenge. As we discussed earlier, if the gap between what they perceive is being demanded of them and their own ability in meeting that demand is widened, motivation to close it may be more difficult.

## GOAL ORIENTATION

Chapter 3 dealt with goal setting and self-management as techniques that can aid learning transfer. In this context, there is a relevant individual personality difference which seems to have a role to play, a difference in what's known as one's goal orientation. Two types of goal orientation are proposed. In learning terms, people with a 'mastery' orientation are focused on developing new skills and determining the most appropriate ways of learning them, that is, achieving mastery. People with a 'performance' orientation are those primarily concerned with performing the task better than (or at least no worse than) others, rather than achieving outright mastery. It has been suggested that motivation to transfer appears to be greater in learners with a mastery orientation, and indeed there is evidence to back this up (Stevens and Gist 1997; Gist and Stevens 1998; Chiaburu and Marinova 2005; Tziner et al. 2007). Mastery-oriented trainees generally engage in a greater variety of activities that will help them maintain taught skills, and exert more effort in their attempts to apply learning. This is not surprising, given that a mastery orientation indicates a stronger concern for skill improvement and suggests that individuals will devote more effort

---

**BOX 5.1: BUILDING CONFIDENCE**

Tim enjoys working for his boss, Jackie. He's particularly pleased with himself today as he has just represented his department (in Jackie's absence) at the annual budget review and has managed to secure for the department a small increase in their budget for the coming year to realize their ambitious plans. It didn't happen overnight, but nevertheless he's very happy with what he's achieved. As a financial person, he's always been comfortable with producing and interpreting figures of any kind. However, when Jackie first suggested to him 2 months ago that he argue the department's case for increased resources at the next annual review he was distinctly nervous.

Luckily for him, Jackie is skilled at coaching and giving feedback. Over the last month or so she has had a number of discussions with him, asking questions, and probing his ideas. He noticed she tended to give him feedback of two sorts. On one hand, she pointed to his experience, his unparalleled knowledge of costs and revenues, and his gently persuasive manner when talking about the subject. On the other hand, she was at pains to point out that the meeting is not one at which the bully wins, but rather where the most coherent argument wins. She even played devil's advocate and got him to argue their case in front of her, an experience which he found a little daunting at first, but ultimately very useful when it came to the real thing.

As a result, he found that the gap he had originally seen between what he felt he was being asked to undertake and his ability to do so was made significantly smaller, which gave him the confidence to take on the challenge. He's now thinking he might try the same thing at the golf club AGM next month...

---

to task performance and enhancement of their skills than will individuals with a performance orientation. It's also suggested that those who are mastery oriented can overcome a lack of motivation due to lower self-efficacy to some extent, as in effect they try harder.

## HOW IT WORKS

The essence of being mastery oriented is that such people want to do things to the very best of their ability. For them, the learning process itself is the reward, and challenges are seen as learning opportunities. Those with a performance orientation tend to be more concerned with how their performance is evaluated in relation to others, and can view challenge less positively, given the potential for failure and thus negative judgements of others.

## TRAINEE CONFIDENCE

Each of the inputs to motivation to learn so far has something to do with the amount of confidence and belief different people have in their ability to make the training work for them. We have already mentioned the term self-efficacy, and will deal with it in greater depth here. Self-efficacy is an important component in motivation overall, playing a major part in determining the amount of effort that will be applied to a task. It is essentially the level of confidence felt by the trainee that they will actually be able either to learn from the training, and/or to apply it afterwards.

Studies of this particular factor have included work by Gist 1989; Gist, Stevens and Bavetta 1991; Stevens and Gist 1997; Warr, Allan and Birdi 1999; Machin and Fogarty 1997, 2003; and Chiaburu and Marinova 2005. The evidence clearly points to a strong relationship between those with higher self-efficacy and better performance following training. The converse is also true, in that people with a higher level of anxiety regarding their ability to transfer learning have performed less well on-the-job afterwards. The studies that produced these results have taken place in a number of different settings, and have looked at the transfer of simple skills such as software application, as well as more complex skills such as negotiation and other skills related to professional development. Indeed Chiaburu and Lindsay (2008) just recently completed a study of 254 employees in a US organization in which trainee self-efficacy has been seen to have a strong effect on motivation to transfer and consequently to learning itself.

## HOW IT WORKS

Given that self-efficacy affects motivation, it's not surprising that it influences learning transfer through its particular effect on motivation to transfer. Like all personal characteristics, different people possess it to differing degrees. In terms of learning, those with higher self-efficacy tend to foresee fewer obstacles to its application back at work, and will tend to report greater confidence concerning their ability to surmount obstacles that might arise. The opposite is the case for those with lower levels. Examples of obstacles cited can be resource issues such as finance and staffing levels, and finding time outside of normal day-to-day operational issues to devise and implement plans.

## WHERE DOES IT COME FROM?

Some people have a high level of self-efficacy in general, and go through life seeing its challenges as opportunities rather than problems. Self-efficacy for those people is probably something they developed early on. Others may have developed it in response to particular challenges they have faced in life, such as the tragic death of a loved one or serious personal trauma. Some will develop it through specific work-related learning experiences, which, over time, give them the confidence as well as the know-how to deal with management problems, both familiar and novel. And finally it's not unknown for people to develop more confidence regarding how to tackle work-based problems through their interaction with other participants on the programme they're attending. This is particularly useful in the context of a longer-term programme, where participants can have the opportunity to try out new things during the life of the programme, and to get feedback on their efforts from facilitators and other participants.

## THE ROLE OF FEEDBACK IN MOTIVATION

Self-efficacy (Bandura 1986) has already been described as the belief that individuals can successfully execute the behaviour required to cope with potentially threatening situations, and we saw that the strength of the belief is a function of the difference between their perception of the demands of those situations, and their perception of their ability to meet those demands. If the gap between the perceptions is too large, they may not be motivated to close it. This is because they believe that they will fail to do so (either because their ability is too low, or the demands too high, or both), and that failure will consequently reduce their self-efficacy further. By not attempting to close the gap in the first place, they can at least maintain their self-efficacy. This response would be typical for example in the case of someone being asked to make a presentation to a large group of people at short notice. They may feel that the demands (preparing at home in their own time, dealing with difficult questions from the audience) are much greater than their ability (other priorities, their fear of standing up in front of groups) and decide to say no, in order not to, as they put it, make a fool of themself. If, on the other hand, the gap is very narrow, or indeed individuals' perception of their ability is greater than their perception of the demands of the task, they will not be motivated to close it either, as doing so does not improve their self-efficacy in any way. In the above example, the same person might decide that the presentation should really be made by one of the juniors.

Perhaps the most important way in which changes in self-efficacy and motivation are enabled is through the feedback process. Feedback can be a very powerful mechanism for changing behaviour. However, the way in which either positive or negative feedback is given is extremely important. Badly given feedback will tend to widen the gap between perceptions of demands and ability discussed above, while properly given feedback should help close it. The following guidelines are worth adhering to, in order to ensure that the giving of feedback will have the desired effect.

- Feedback should be intended to be helpful.

- Feedback should be given directly to the person, face to face.

- Feedback should be specific rather than general.

- Feedback should always describe facts or behaviours, rather than being seen to make any judgement of a person.

- Feedback should focus on the effects of the behaviour.

- Feedback should be given when the person appears ready to accept it.

- Feedback should include only things that the person can do something about.

- Feedback should never cover more issues than a person can handle at any one time.

- Finally, properly given feedback should give people the opportunity to check that they have understood it properly.

## Motivation to Transfer

Much of the research conducted has concluded that a major effect on motivation to transfer is from a trainee's motivation to learn. Both of these are influenced by the personal characteristics discussed in this chapter. There are a number of other influences on motivation to transfer. These include some training design factors, and factors in the work environment such as manager support and coaching, as well as peer and organizational support, discussed in earlier chapters.

In general, people with high degrees of motivation to transfer are characterized by:

- A readiness to learn. They tend to keep an open mind, and see work and other challenges as opportunities to learn.

- They are likely to have identified a particular training or development need which the intervention they have just attended was designed to address. They can also see opportunities to use their learning, and feel it will make a difference to their job.

- They have made use of the network of co-attendees on the programme to test ideas, offer and receive advice, and use it as a source of support following the programme.

- They have a high degree of confidence in their ability to make use of their learning to initiate change within their areas of responsibility.

- Their work environments, and in particular their immediate boss, are supportive of learning.

- They tend to see their involvement in training and development as developmental rather than remedial.

## Ability to Transfer

With a better understanding of motivation, we can now turn our attention to that all-important piece of the process – how to turn all the motivation to learn and to transfer that has been generated into action, and finally 'make it happen'. Of course all the motivation in the world will not ensure learning transfer happens if the opportunities are not there to make it happen. Work environments can seem a little like 'black holes', those spaces into which much energy disappears and from which little or none emerges. As stated at the start of this book, very little, it would seem, of the vast amount of resources spent on training and development activity results in tangible and meaningful benefits for organizations. While all of the factors discussed so far have an important role to play in enabling transfer, a recent study by this author (Kirwan 2005a) would seem to suggest that the single most important characteristic is the presence (or generation) of a personal ability to transfer – making the 'time and space' to enable transfer. Conducted around a management development programme within the Irish health service, the study highlighted the particular importance of two factors – the participants' *motivation to transfer* (as predicted), but also their *personal ability to transfer*. As we saw, *motivation to transfer* is the strength and persistence of effort in using learned knowledge and skills back at work, whilst *personal ability to transfer* is the extent to which individuals can make the time and 'mental space' in their work to apply that learning. Within the study, the latter factor was seen as the more important. In fact, of all the transfer factors studied, it was the one that correlated most strongly and significantly with actual learning transfer.

## WHAT THE LITERATURE SAYS

Surprisingly, the literature on one's personal ability to transfer, an important factor in its own right, is quite thin. However, its constituent elements can be found in other influences on learning transfer. In particular, these are the factors already discussed in Chapter 3 concerning the formation of the 'bridge' between the classroom and the workplace. As such, they will not be discussed further here. However in summary, activities such as goal setting, self-management and coaching are all regarded as important elements in generating the time and mental space needed to establish new behaviour following a training or development experience.

It would appear that those who score highly on *ability to transfer* (Kirwan 2005b) are those who have:

- the motivation to transfer;

- the ability and/or opportunity to reflect on learning, including new knowledge, skills or other learning, in order to see how that learning can be used;

- competence in goal setting and self-management;

- assertiveness, and being able to say 'no' when necessary;

- autonomy in their jobs, and being able to use it to 'make things happen'.

In addition, support from a number of other sources may help – from their manager, in the form of coaching, feedback and guidance; from their peers, such as 'filling in the gaps' while they're away training, as well as providing feedback on new ideas; and from their organization, in terms of providing opportunities to apply the learning at work, and follow-up support. All of these influences were already discussed in earlier chapters.

## HOW DOES IT WORK?

One of the most important ways in which individuals can make that mental space for themselves is through the process of reflection. Reflection as a facilitating factor in transfer appears in the use of such tools as self-management (Brown and Latham 2000), relapse prevention (Burke 1997) and coaching (Sloan 2001). Being able to reflect on what you learn on a programme and making changes to your behaviour is seen as an important part of making the training work. However, as almost anyone will tell you, finding time to do this is never easy. Many work environments are not at all conducive to such a practice. So people tend to find opportunities to think in other places and at other times, such as at home, while driving or in the garden. They can then think about how they might put a newly acquired skill into practice or how they handled its application and how they might have done it better. Another way in which time and space can be created is by using one's peers. Peers can cover for an individual while the latter spends time on a future-oriented application of learning, such as a redesign of the appraisal system, or the writing of a service plan. Indeed a peer who has attended a similar programme, or better still, the same programme, will be able to offer more options in this regard, including discussion around application of learning and giving feedback. Finally, using those in a network that has built up around a programme will provide still further options for discussion, support and feedback.

For those who may not have a high degree of support around them to help them reflect and practise, it seems that the degree to which they are assertive can make a difference. Assertive people tend to be very clear about what they want to do (for example introduce a change in working methods), and are good at sticking to it. In particular, those who are good at saying 'no' to others when necessary find it less difficult to make the time to reflect. Others just have to work harder at it. For those who are not particularly assertive, all is still not lost. Research has demonstrated that the degree of autonomy people have in their jobs is a critical contributor to increasing their personal ability to transfer. On balance then, where an individual's ability to transfer is not a characteristic they naturally possess, more autonomy in their jobs will make it less likely that this will be a barrier.

## In Practice

### WORK ON EXPECTANCIES

Given the factors that affect one's motivation to learn, one of the principal ways in which it can be activated or indeed tested is via a discussion with the boss prior to attending a programme. This discussion can fulfil a number of requirements. There is the matter of bringing the boss 'into the loop' in the first place. In far too many organizations still, managers see training as something that should be left to the training department, and see pre-training discussions with staff as a luxury for which they don't have the time. However, as the evidence shows, nothing could be further from the truth. At the meeting, questions such as the following should be discussed:

- Why should the trainee attend the programme?

- What do they hope to learn?

- Is there a different or better way to learn it?

- How will they apply what they learned when they come back to work?

- What difference will application of their learning make?

- How can the boss help?

By airing the issues around these questions, the boss and the trainee can between them agree the best course of action. Sometimes, indeed, the best course of action may be for the trainee not to attend the particular proposed programme, and instead meet their needs in another way.

## WORK ON CONFIDENCE

While not much can be done about this if the individual has a generally low level of self-efficacy, it may be that their perceptions regarding their ability or the demands of application are inaccurate. Effective feedback (part of the manager's role as coach) will do much to reassure them (if that's what is necessary) and encourage them to take on the challenge that using the learning entails.

## WORK ON LOCUS OF CONTROL

Once again, locus of control is a personal characteristic. Nevertheless, working on an individual's confidence through helping them generate appropriate attributions can be very beneficial. It is also something that effective coaches do. Encouraging individuals to take credit for their achievements, generating internal attributions for success ('the presentation went well because you prepared well') or indeed to write off unsuccessful episodes to experience, generating external attributions for failure ('the person who asked that question has a particular issue with our strategy for the future') in order to maintain their self-efficacy will help to sustain their motivation to learn and to use what they learn.

## WORK ON GOALS

We saw earlier that people with a mastery goal orientation will be more likely to transfer learning. During the process of action planning and goal setting, encouraging them to set goals that achieve mastery of the task to be applied will be of some help in this regard. Achieving mastery may require some degree of overlearning (discussed in Chapter 2) and so significant opportunity to practise a new skill or competence and receive appropriate feedback should be built in to the plan.

## WORK ON COMMITMENT

We also saw earlier that those people who demonstrate higher levels of organizational commitment and have more positive job attitudes tend to make better use of the training they get. One of the many fine lines that managers have to walk is the one between closing gaps in skill needs and providing learning opportunities as a reward or some sort of motivator. It's clear that undertaking training or development can be rewarding for individuals. However this will only be the case if such an event is what the individual wants and is in keeping with their development needs. Therefore, how the invitation to attend is presented is important. It will be better if it is seen more as a future-oriented developmental opportunity, which is intended to build on competence they already have, and less as a means of remedying some deficiency.

## USE YOUR PEERS

Depending on the closeness of the relationship and level of dependency between team members, one's peers can be a source of support, either from the point of view of being a sounding board when reflecting, or as a practical support for the implementation of new ideas.

## GET A COACH

The benefits of well-directed coaching have been described and discussed in detail in Chapter 3. In reality, what a coach (whether internal or external to the organization) can do is to help create that necessary time and mental space, reality test initiatives and offer sound advice based on experience.

## MAKE TIME TO REFLECT

Although most working lives allow little time to just sit and reflect, the evidence clearly shows that finding the time to do this is a worthwhile investment. It's an essential stage in the learning cycle, and has the advantage of being able to be conducted anywhere. Issues to be thought about could include how a particular skill might be applied back at work or how a piece of knowledge might be adapted to one's particular situation. Reflecting on an experience as part of an effort to improve a particular skill could include questions such as: What was the situation? What were my thoughts, feelings? What did I want to do? What did I actually do? What was the result? What did the experience teach me?

---

### BOX 5.2: THE VALUE OF REFLECTION

It takes some assertiveness, when faced with a room full of busy managers, anxious to 'start the real work' as soon as they leave your classroom, to get them to spend time in reflecting on what they've learned in order to help them transfer it back to work. As people who tend to put a higher value on doing rather than thinking, they are often understandably reluctant. Yet research on learning has taught us that a vital component of learning from experience is developing insights from past events and applying them to future actions. This cannot take place without reflection, and the classroom may realistically be the last opportunity they have to engage in it.

Managers usually learn to solve problems at work by first articulating what they think the problem is. They then analyze the factors contributing to the problem, formulate a response based on some framework or theory, and try it out in practice. All of these steps require reflection. However, with most management problems this is done unconsciously. On the other hand, many of the issues that arise in management development programmes (for example, how to motivate a team that is performing well below par), are more complex and require more conscious processing.

There are ways of making this easier for those managers. For those particularly uncomfortable with individual reflection, other options are using a coach (which may be another participant on the programme) or conducting the reflection in a group. In either case, a set of questions can be provided which gives a structure to the process and enhances the probability of success.

---

## CONSTRUCT A PERSONAL DEVELOPMENT PLAN (PDP)

The idea behind PDPs is that they provide a specific development solution based on clearly identified needs, and allow for a range of appropriate development methods. Key features of PDPs are that learning takes place in its natural (work) setting, and in a way that suits the learning style(s) of the learner. Learning through the formation and implementation of PDPs is usually most effective when it engages all phases of the learning cycle. Once a goal has been set, the individual embarks on achieving it (using a variety of practical means), reflects on progress, forms frameworks and concepts about what does or doesn't work, and tries it out again. To take an example, a manager may decide (or agree) that improving their skill in negotiating is important for them to undertake. Formulating a PDP around this need would probably include:

- A clear assessment of their capability in that regard. The assessment could come from reflection on their need for the skill (possibly as an outcome of a negative experience), or it could come from feedback arising informally or from an appraisal process. Concrete evidence should be sought in order to be clear about actual performance.

- A specific goal to be reached. This might comprise the conclusion of a successful negotiation at some time in the future, and/or a general improvement in the skill over time. In each case, concrete evidence to measure improvement and/or achievement of the goal needs to be gathered.

- An appropriate strategy or set of strategies to reach this goal. This is where the particular flexibility of a PDP becomes an advantage, taking account of learners' different learning styles. For example, to increase their level of skill in negotiating, the manager might do one or more of the following:
    - read and reflect on books or journal articles on the subject;
    - talk to (and learn from) people whom they regard as skilled negotiators;
    - watch those people in action;
    - attend a training course in negotiation skills;
    - practise the appropriate skills in a 'safe' environment with a colleague.

It can be seen that one of the benefits of this type of process is its flexibility. It can be engaged in any time, and can be a longer or shorter process. It goes without saying that for it to be of benefit it should be engaged in on an ongoing basis, especially as things change so fast in the workplace. It should be used in conjunction with the reflective process outlined above.

## USE A LEARNING LOG

One of the tools than can help maintain a PDP, and encourage a disciplined approach to learning from events that occur at work, is a learning log. A typical use of a learning log for individuals in the context of PDP is to focus on what happened, what reflection they have engaged in as a result, what conclusions they have come to and what future actions they want to take as a result. Keeping a learning log at any time, but particularly when developing a particular skill can be very beneficial.

## Summary

As we have seen in this chapter, the literature concerning personal characteristics that can affect learning transfer has focused a lot of its attention on their effect on motivation to learn and motivation to transfer learning. It is clear that motivation plays a major part. In this regard, the trainees' self-efficacy and their expectancies have an important role to play. Motivation is also affected by work environment factors, which have already been discussed. Different individual characteristics such as organizational commitment and job involvement exert varying effects. Where they have been studied, personality factors such as locus of control and goal orientation have clearly demonstrated effects. Finally, some relevant cognitive style differences have been identified.

In turn, motivation to transfer is the biggest single influence on ability to transfer. Like motivation to transfer, personal ability to transfer is quite a personal characteristic, although we have seen it can be influenced by other factors. Those who demonstrate a high level of personal ability to transfer provide strong evidence for a personal responsibility for 'making transfer happen', and the use of one's autonomy, one's peers and one's own time if necessary in order to achieve this.

## References

Adams, J.S. (1963). Toward an understanding of inequity. *Journal of Abnormal Social Psychology*, 67, 422–36.

Baldwin, T.T., Magjuka, R.J. and Loher, B.T. (1991). The perils of participation: Effects of choice of training on trainee motivation and learning. *Personnel Psychology*, 44, 51–65.

Bandura, A. (1986). *Social foundations of thought and action*. Englewood Cliffs, NJ: Prentice Hall.

Baumgartel, H. and Jeanpierre, F. (1972). Applying new knowledge in the back-home setting: A study of Indian managers' adoptive efforts. *Journal of Applied Behavioural Science*, 8, 674–94.

Baumgartel, H., Reynolds, M. and Pathan, R. (1984). How personality and organization-climate variables moderate the effectiveness of management development programmes: A review and some recent research findings. *Management and Labour Studies*, 9, 1–16.

Brown, T.C. and Latham, G.P. (2000). The effects of goal setting and self-instruction training on the performance of unionized employees. *Relations Industrielles*, 55(1), 80–95.

Burke, L.A. (1997). Improving positive transfer: A test of relapse prevention training on transfer outcomes. *Human Resource Development Quarterly*, 8(2), 115–28.

Cheng, E.W.L. (2000). Test of the MBA knowledge and skills transfer. *International Journal of Human Resource Management*, 11(4), 837–52.

Chiaburu, D.S. and Lindsay, D.R. (2008). Can do or will do? The importance of self efficacy and instrumentality for training transfer. *Human Resource Development International*, 11(2), 199–206.

Chiaburu, D.S. and Marinova, S.V. (2005). What predicts skill transfer? An exploratory study of goal orientation, self efficacy and organizational supports. *International Journal of Training and Development*, 9(2), 110–23.

Clark, C.S., Dobbins, G.H. and Ladd, R.T. (1993). Exploratory field study of training motivation: Influence of involvement, credibility, and transfer climate. *Group and Organization Management*, 18(3), 292–307.

Facteau, J.D., Dobbins, G.H., Russell, J.E.A., Ladd, R.T. and Kudisch, J.D. (1995). The influence of general perceptions of the training environment on pretraining motivation and perceived training transfer. *Journal of Management*, 21, 1–25.

Gist, M.E. (1989). The influence of training method on self efficacy and idea generation among managers. *Personnel Psychology*, 42, 787–805.

Gist, M.E. and Stevens, C.K. (1998). Effects of practice conditions and supplemental training method on cognitive learning and interpersonal skill generalization. *Organizational Behavior and Human Decision Processes*, 75(2), 142–69.

Gist, M.E., Stevens, C.K. and Bavetta, A.G. (1991). Effects of self-efficacy and post-training intervention on the acquisition and maintenance of complex interpersonal skills. *Personnel Psychology*, 44, 837–61.

Heider, F. (1958). *The psychology of interpersonal relations.* New York: Wiley.

Herzberg, F. (1968). One more time: How do you motivate employees? *Harvard Business Review*, 46, 53–62.

Hicks, W.D. and Klimowski, R.J. (1987). Entry into training programs and its effects on training outcomes: A field experiment. *Academy of Management Journal*, 30, 542–52.

Huczynski, A.A. and Lewis, J.W. (1980). An empirical study into the learning transfer process in management training. *Journal of Management Studies*, 17, 227–40.

Kelly, G. (1955). *The psychology of personal constructs.* New York: Norton.

Kirwan, C. (2005a). *Transfer of learning: Understanding the process and test of a model.* Unpublished doctoral thesis. Henley Management College/Brunel University.

Kirwan, C. (2005b). Management development's black holes: A question of time and space. *People Focus* 3(1), 26–7.

Machin, M.A. and Fogarty, G.J. (1997). The effects of self efficacy, motivation to transfer, and situational constraints on transfer intentions and transfer of training. *Performance Improvement Quarterly*, 10, 98–115.

Machin, A. and Fogarty, G.J. (2003). Perceptions of training-related factors and personal variables as predictors of transfer implementation intentions. *Journal of Business and Psychology*, 18(1), 51–71.

Noe, R.A. and Schmitt, N. (1986). The influence of trainee attitudes on training effectiveness: Test of a model. *Personnel Psychology*, 39, 497–523.

Sloan, E.B. (2001). *The contribution of university-based executive education to corporate executive talent management results.* Joint research project conducted by the international university consortium for executive education (UNICON) and Personnel Decisions International. Minneapolis: Personnel Decisions International. In K. Kraiger (Ed.), *Creating, implementing, and managing effective training and development: State-of-the-art lessons for practice.* San Francisco: Jossey-Bass.

Stevens, C.K. and Gist, M.E. (1997). Effects of self efficacy and goal-orientation training on interpersonal skill maintenance: What are the mechanisms? *Personnel Psychology*, 50(4), 955–78.

Tannenbaum, S.I., Mathieu, J.E., Salas, E. and Cannon-Bowers, J.B. (1991). Meeting trainees' expectations: The influence of training fulfilment on the development of commitment, self efficacy, and motivation. *Journal of Applied Psychology*, 76, 759–69.

Tesluk, P.E., Farr, J.L., Mathieu, J.E. and Vance, R.J. (1995). Generalization of employee involvement training to the job setting: Individual and situational effects. *Personnel Psychology*, 48, 607–32.

Tziner, A., Fisher, M., Senior, T. and Weisberg, J. (2007). Effects of trainee characteristics on training effectiveness. *International Journal of Selection and Assessment*, 15(2), 167–74.

Vroom, V. (1964). *Work and motivation.* New York: Wiley.

Warr, P.B., Allan, C. and Birdi, K. (1999). Predicting three levels of training outcome. *Journal of Occupational and Organizational Psychology*, 72, 351–76.

# 6

# Dealing with Resistance

## Introduction

The chapters that have gone before have been full of good advice, gathered from reputable sources, on how you can make the most of your organization's learning and development efforts. On a local level, the building of a climate for transfer through good management practice, creating a set of conditions in which colleagues and the organization in general work together to ensure the investment in learning efforts is optimized, is of course a major contributor. At a broader level, the building of what we can call 'learning organizations' (although still a dream for people in most organizations) will further enhance learning capability.

So why doesn't it work? If all the interested parties believe that learning is a good thing, why is it so hard to become a 'learning organization'? At the top, for instance, its management wants to ensure that the skills, knowledge and other abilities it requires now and into the future are readily accessible. Further down, the bulk of employees want to know that opportunities for them to move up (or move on) are available to them. Yet real learning organizations are hard to find, and the often conflicting interests of a range of stakeholders – those who have an interest in the inputs, processes or outcomes of learning and development activities – make real learning transfer hard to achieve.

## How Would We Recognize a Learning Organization?

Perhaps the answer may lie in the definition of a learning organization. Although clear and concise definitions are hard to come by, the following, from Garvin (1993, 80) seems to fit the bill. He defines it as 'an organization skilled at creating, acquiring and transferring knowledge, and at modifying its behaviour to reflect new knowledge and insights'. Thus organizations that can lay claim to the title need not only to be able to generate new knowledge, but to use it in a practical way, to practise what they preach, as it were. This is not as easy as it sounds. Many organizations for example are in a position to generate new knowledge – from customers, from the collective wisdom of their members or from the world at large – yet in reality do not use this information as well as they might. Garvin would see the ability to transfer knowledge quickly around the organization as one of the key components of a learning organization. Another is the ability to experiment and learn from experience. Indeed the two practices go together, and it is probably in this arena that improvements in the practice of learning transfer most closely affect organizations' ability to become learning organizations.

So, what is it that prevents them? To help explain, Dipboye (1997) offers some initial observations on why organizations fail to adopt and implement what the organizational literature would describe as effective training practices. He believes organizations:

- don't implement an integrated systems design model in their training;

- don't assess training and development needs;

- rarely evaluate their training programmes rigorously;

- often make irrational decisions about training;

- allow fads and fashions to dominate their training.

All of the above conditions have implications for the generalization and maintenance of learning. For instance, best practice training design factors discussed in Chapter 2 are part of an integrated systems design model. The importance of both accurate analysis of training needs and rigorous evaluation to determine whether they are being met has also been highlighted. In addition, anyone who has been on the receiving end of decisions made in some organizations regarding what training is supported and how it gets carried out will testify to many an inconsistency. Lastly, the success of bestsellers that fill airport bookshelves everywhere can be a clear indication of the latest fad. The fact that they are often on sale at half price within weeks can be an equally clear indication of how short-lived some of them are, and suggests that real answers are not as easy to find as some would have us believe. Allied to the factors already identified in Chapter 4 by Clarke (2002), such as heavy workloads, time pressures and lack of reinforcement of training, we can see that there are a lot of pressures operating against successful learning transfer. It would seem that despite the broader, more strategic agreement around the needs of the organization, in the short term the needs of one group may directly clash with the needs of others, with the resultant negative consequences for the application and spread of new knowledge.

## The Stakeholders

Who then are the primary stakeholders, and what are their primary concerns? Within the organization, they comprise senior management, managers and supervisors of trainees, peers of trainees and the trainees themselves. We can also add trainers and consultants, whether they operate from inside or outside the organization. Whilst we can agree that in the long term their needs overlap and indeed sometimes coincide, the reality of organizational life is such that in the short term they do not. Senior management, for example, need to be concerned with what they spend and what they get in return, and in the face of many competing demands, may focus more on what they can measure easily. It's also quite common that they lack the detailed knowledge necessary (a problem exacerbated if they don't recognize the limitations of their knowledge) to clearly understand the long-term value of learning and development. Organizational politics may also play a part. Senior managers may have a need to 'look good' in front of others, restricting their enthusiasm for longer term, risky issues such as people development. The pressure for results is also felt further down the organization, making the achievement of departmental goals on time and within budget a priority for middle managers and team leaders to achieve, leaving less room for the important but less urgent tasks such as people development. The individual focus and competitive nature of some departmental units may also mean that peers feel that supporting others in their learning efforts may detract from achievement of their own goals. Finally, those consultants on whom organizations depend for advice and direction may be limited in what they can offer, choosing to do what they know, rather than (really) knowing what they do.

In addition to 'not being a learning organization' two other organizational-level factors may work against the transfer and maintenance of new learning from training and development initiatives. The first of these is the organization's culture, while the second, perhaps not unrelated, is the extent of political behaviour and use of power that exists.

## Organization Culture

Frameworks to characterize organization culture have been described by many authors. While in-depth treatment of their content is not appropriate here, culture tends to be defined within these frameworks in terms of a number of recurring dimensions. For example Harrison (1972) describes four orientations towards power, the role, the task and the person respectively while Quinn and Rohrbaugh (1983) place the emphases on the four areas of support, innovation, rules and goals.

Given organizations' concern with developing and maintaining appropriate cultures it makes sense to have a look at what features of an organization's culture might help or hinder the application of new learning. A good checklist for looking at how cultures are maintained is provided by Hellriegel, Slocum and Woodman (1992). Whatever the framework used, they suggest five mechanisms, all of which can have implications for the promotion and use of learning within the organization:

1.   what managers pay attention to, measure and control;

2.   the ways in which managers (particularly top management) react to critical incidents and organizational crises;

3.   managerial role modelling, teaching and coaching;

4.   criteria for allocating rewards and status;

5.   criteria for recruitment, selection, promotion and removal from the organization.

Depending on the culture of the organization, different signals can be sent out to indicate what's seen as important. If it values learning, then the importance of people development, for example, will be apparent in its performance management processes and in the rewards (such as promotion) for managers who do it well. Similarly, should a crisis arise, such as a major slowdown in business, whether the organization starts making people redundant straight away or starts to consider other opportunities in order to retain them might also indicate something about the value it places on its human resources. On the other hand, in strongly task or goal-oriented cultures, for instance, managers must ensure that organizational objectives such as project deadlines and milestones are met on time and within budgets. This, according to Quinn and Rohrbaugh, competes directly with their role in managing the efforts of a range of people and their responsibility to ensure that the talents of those people are developed for the benefit of themselves and the organization.

## Power and Politics

It's also reasonable to assume that there is a relationship between the culture of the organization and where power is distributed in that organization. Thus in task and goal-focused cultures, it is likely that greater power will be in the hands of those who are seen to be good at 'getting the job done', with less emphasis on how they actually do so. Similarly, in people-focused cultures, where personal development is a key feature, those who have a reputation for developing effective teams and who communicate well will find it easier to rise to positions of particular influence. It's hard to be precise about how this affects learning transfer, but evidence from Chapter 4 indicates that work environments (which are often, though not always, strongly influenced by the dominant organizational culture) that inhibit learning transfer are those where work overload and a focus on short-term goals mitigate against people finding the time to reflect on and experiment with new learning.

The ways in which the use (or indeed abuse) of power can affect learning transfer tend to be in the areas of access to knowledge, control over resources and power in decision making (Daft 1992). Thus if the person in a position of power takes the view that the less knowledge is shared, the better for their position, then knowledge will not be shared. If they feel resources that are needed to manage the transfer of knowledge around the organization could better be used elsewhere, then knowledge will not be transferred. Decisions made on these issues will have important implications for transfer.

## Local Resistance

At a more local level, resistance to application of learning can come from a number of sources. In the same way as we saw earlier that support can come from managers, peers and the organization, so it is with resistance. We'll look at each of these now.

### THE UNHELPFUL MANAGER

Perhaps the most important influence outside of individuals themselves is their manager. The extent to which individuals get neutral or negative responses from their manager when applying skills learned in training can have a significant effect. As seen in Chapter 4, for those managers who are considered unsupportive, their behaviour can perhaps be placed in one of two categories – indifference or active resistance. Indifference is perhaps more common. Some managers are indifferent to the development of skills (other than technical skills) in general, especially from formal training, coming as they may from the 'old school' of management, or perhaps from a background that is more used to dealing in certainties and tangible outcomes. Their reaction to participants returning from a programme may just be to ignore it, not asking how they got on or how the learning might be used. Or if they feel a little uncomfortable, perhaps even a little threatened, they may make fun of 'business school' ideas. It's also not unusual for managers to have their own priorities, which may conflict with those of the participants. Sometimes they may feel a sense of loss of control resulting from application of new learning and ideas that are not their own. Their response might be to keep tight control on things themselves, restricting the amount of involvement or feedback, or in extreme cases taking new ideas from the participant and passing them off as their own. Overall, these barriers can have several net effects. Firstly, there is a loss to the workplace of new knowledge, skills and attitudes through managers not supporting their maintenance and development. Secondly, this in turn can reduce the motivation to transfer, as prospects of success will start to seem further away. Thirdly, a significant amount of energy is wasted in trying to bypass these managers, energy which could be put to more productive use.

Indeed people can be very inventive when they need to find a way around these barriers. A quite common strategy is to 'sidestep' the manager in question, although this is perhaps easier to do in areas where shift working is in operation, and participants might actually have more than one boss. Another strategy, recommended by time management gurus everywhere is to act first and report after the event, based on the premise that it's easier to beg forgiveness than to seek permission!

## THE UNHELPFUL PEERS

Peers can also be indifferent or indeed resistant. One of the main reasons this might happen is where personality or work styles differ markedly. However, a competitive environment such as a sales environment may also encourage peers to compete against each other in the interests of overall unit performance. While this can have positive effects, it can also contribute to a climate of mistrust, where others' motives for helping might be seen as suspect. Environments

---

**BOX 6.1: WHY BOTHER?**

Jack is really beginning to get fed up. He's a team leader in the recruitment section of a large food processing company, which he joined straight from college. Although he's there only 6 months, it's long enough for him to see a number of things that in his view need 'shaking up'. This view has strengthened since his return from a very useful seminar he attended recently about *'What's new in recruitment and selection'*. It gave him a number of ideas that he'd like to put into practice here, in particular the increased use of online recruitment, and the introduction of some specialized ability tests which he's convinced would shorten the selection process and result in better skilled recruits.

It's not easy, though. The team, which has been in place a long time, is very comfortable with (and quite skilled at, it must be said) the current routine. None of them has any qualifications in ability testing, believing that meeting people face to face is the only way to determine if they're right for the job. Besides, the trips to larger population centres around for the summer recruitment campaigns are a pleasant distraction. In addition, both Jack's predecessor and his current boss have worked as members of the team in the past. He has tried raising the issue several times, outlining the possibilities both for improved performance of the unit, and (he believes) a greater level of motivation amongst the members of the team from an increase in their range of knowledge and skills. His boss, while he listens to his ideas ('my door is always open') hasn't actually said he'll do anything about it. Still, there's more than one employer in town...

---

such as this also are characterized by a lack of interdependency, which further reduces the need for collaboration.

## THE UNHELPFUL WORK ENVIRONMENT

We also saw in Chapter 4 that when discussing the organizational climate for learning transfer, more barriers than facilitators are typically identified. The evidence certainly suggests that resistance to change in the work environment plays a role in influencing transfer, and that the role of the manager (for good or ill) is a central one. There can be an enormous difference in the climate created by (sometimes) young, dynamic managers and staff with new ideas on the one hand, and (sometimes) older, more settled, more traditional managers and staff on the other. Environments managed by the latter tend not to have either a broad or a long-term outlook, whereas the former can be a rich source of new ideas and enthusiasm for change. Such work environments have been described in studies by Peters and O'Connor (1980) and Clarke (2002). Investigation of their collective resistance to change and its effects suggests that it tends to revolve around a number of key fears, particularly, though not exclusively, held by managers at all levels in these environments. There is a belief that:

*Managers' responsibility is being eroded*   Fears expressed in this regard tend to reflect a concern that a 'new style of managing' (that is, less directive and more participative) will result in a diminution of the influence of those with responsibility for managing others. Managers with this point of view are likely to value experience (if gained over a long number of years, so much the better) over innovation or creativity, and place a strong emphasis on position within the organization.

*Management is becoming too complicated*    It's also common to find perceptions in some quarters that management is becoming too complicated, with perhaps too much attention being given to the feelings and aspirations of staff members (a people-oriented environment) instead of concentrating on the tasks to be done (a task-oriented environment).

*Managers aren't being allowed to manage*   The fears and concerns already described above by the managers also manifest themselves in a concern that their own skills and abilities might not count as much in the future.

Overall, some or all of the above conditions could combine to generate the fears expressed. It is true that the world of management has undergone significant change in a relatively short space of time, with new structures, changing roles, higher levels of accountability and greater use of technology. The impact of this growing burden on those who might already feel less able to cope could well be to react defensively against it in order to maintain their self-efficacy and not 'show themselves up', manifesting itself in their lack of enthusiasm for change.

## FACILITATING CHANGE

On the other side of the coin, experience has demonstrated that a number of conditions in the work environment will, if they exist, balance the transfer-inhibiting effects of the type of work climate just described. Within work environments, resistance to transfer can be overcome by:

*Openness*   A regular flow of information in all directions will ensure people are better placed to cope with changes in the way of working brought about by, among other things, the application of new learning.

*Communication and meetings*   The demonstration of openness through the involvement of staff in meetings and decisions affecting them lowers resistance to change, and improves the flow of new ideas. Frequent one-to-one meetings and availability of managers to discuss change issues are also contributing factors.

*Using experience*   The most change-oriented environments use the experience of all the members of staff, and manage to develop more of a 'team spirit'.

## In Practice

As the reasons for resistance to learning transfer are many and varied, so too are the ways in which this resistance might be overcome.

### ENCOURAGE BUY-IN AT APPROPRIATE LEVELS

This instruction has probably become something of a cliché over the years. Yet despite the exhortations, far too many training and development initiatives are developed and implemented in isolation from the running of the business. The levels we're talking about may be at participant level, at manager/supervisor level, and at senior manager level where the initiative might be likely to have organization-wide implications. We can look at each in turn.

*At participant level*   We have already seen some implications for learning transfer of the involvement of participants in the identification of learning needs and programme content where appropriate. Any consultation undertaken at this level will pay dividends later on.

*At manager/supervisor level*   The importance of their role has been highlighted in Chapter 4. People at this level need to be involved throughout the entire learning process. Their input can be valuable at the training needs assessment stage. It is also important that they meet with the participant before the programme to discuss desired learning outcomes and how they might be used. They also need to meet afterwards, to begin implementation of the action plan and provide coaching, feedback and support.

*At senior management level*   There may be a need to reinforce the message that a particular learning intervention is trying to promote. Senior managers can send out strong messages (sometimes inadvertently) about what's seen as important.

They should channel this influence and be role models for the change.

## MAKE A BUSINESS CASE FOR THE INTERVENTION

Learning and development interventions are in effect change interventions. Therefore guidelines for best practice in change management should apply. One of the most critical is that the change is seen to be necessary. As far as possible, the need should be expressed in business terms. Even if this can't be quantified in financial terms, at least some indication of the expected effects on organizational performance should be described.

## ADOPT ADULT LEARNING PRINCIPLES

It's true that many people in the workforce do not have fond memories of being in classrooms. Mention training to them and these memories come flooding back – learning things they can't see the point of, and trying to remember things they'd much sooner forget. One way of easing this trauma is to use a learning process that makes use of what they already know, and build on it by using their own experience. The value of using adult learning principles was discussed in Chapter 2, and the benefits of a constructivist approach to learning have been demonstrated in the literature. The use of this approach can play an important part in decreasing resistance and demonstrating that learning can happen in many, non-threatening ways.

## TREAT THE ORGANIZATION'S LEARNING DISABILITIES

Many organizations have what can be regarded as 'organizational learning disabilities', characteristics of the organization that make it difficult to see what learning opportunities exist, but also what learning opportunities they may be missing. Garvin (2000) cites three principal disabilities – biased information; flawed interpretation of that information; and inaction. Any of these will inhibit the spread of real information that can be used for learning throughout the organization.

## Summary

As with change of any description, using applications of new learning to bring about change in the workplace can have its difficulties. Old habits may have to be broken and real or imagined fears allayed. Even where the relevant stakeholders are in agreement regarding the need, they may differ strongly in their view as to how that need should be met. Issues such as the culture of the organization, the location of power and the action of influential individuals can work for or against the transfer of learning throughout that organization. It's probably true that work environments don't actually exhibit outright resistance to transfer, but it does seem from the evidence that many of them exhibit a high level of indifference to it. Perhaps this is a demonstration of the difference between espoused theory (Argyris, 1982), in which organizations acknowledge that training is a good thing; and their theory in use, where in actuality they do nothing active to facilitate its transfer to the workplace.

## References

Argyris, C. (1982). *Reasoning, learning and action.* San Francisco: Jossey-Bass.

Clarke, N. (2002). Job/work environment factors influencing training transfer within a human service agency: Some indicative support for Baldwin and Ford's transfer climate construct. *International Journal of Training and Development,* 6(3), 146–62.

Daft, R.L. (1992*). Organization theory and design.* 4$^{th}$ ed. St. Paul: West Publishing.

Dipboye, R.L. (1997). Organizational barriers to implementing a rational model of training. In M.A. Quinones & A. Ehrenstein (eds.), *Training for a rapidly changing workplace: Applications of psychological research.* (pp. 31–60). Washington, DC: American Psychological Association.

Garvin, D.A. (1993). Building a learning organization. *Harvard Business Review, July–August,* 78–91.

Garvin, D.A. (2000). *Learning in action.* Boston: HBS.

Harrison, R. (1972). Understanding your organization's character. *Harvard Business Review,* 50(3), 119–28.

Hellriegel, D., Slocum Jr, J.W. and Woodman, R.W. (1992). *Organizational behaviour.* 6$^{th}$ ed. St. Paul: West Publishing.

Peters, L.H. and O'Connor, E.J. (1980). Situational constraints and work outcomes: The influences of a frequently overlooked construct. *Academy of Management Review,* 5, 391–98.

Quinn, R.E. and Rohrbaugh, J. (1983). A spatial model of effectiveness criteria: Towards a competing values approach. *Management Science,* 29(3), 363–77.

# 7

# Measuring Learning Outcomes

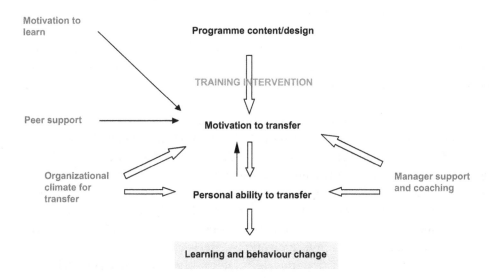

## Introduction

One of the biggest challenges facing people in training and learning departments is demonstrating to others that what they're doing makes a tangible difference to the organization. In some organizations, this is an integral part of the way they operate. In others, such evidence of effectiveness is not so actively sought. What's not untypical in these cases is that the management of the organization make the assumption that if they're spending the same as everyone else (typically between one per cent and five per cent of payroll) they're doing all right. However, this focus on input rather than output has a serious drawback. In the absence of evidence that the resources are being spent wisely, when times are tight the training and development budget is likely to go the way of the sports and social budget or the charity contribution – 'it's nice to have if we can afford it, but we've got to prioritise…' On the other hand, organizations that have a strong culture of measurement, such as manufacturing companies, may be in the habit of always wanting to see hard evidence of the results of their efforts. However, this too has a potential drawback where training and development are concerned. If their emphasis on hard measurement is too strong, they run the risk of measuring only that which is easy to measure in concrete terms rather than what is of most relevance. So, deciding what should be measured and how it should be measured, and finding the right balance between the alternatives available is a matter that requires some serious thought.

## Evaluation Frameworks

Over the decades, different frameworks for the measurement of training outcomes have been used, amongst which a number of similarities exist. The CIRO approach from Warr, Bird and Rackham (1970) looks at evaluation across a broad range of factors and includes evaluation of *context* (evaluation of immediate, intermediate and ultimate objectives); *input* (examines the relative merits of different training methods, such as whether it should be conducted internally or externally, or whether it should include or exclude line management); *reaction* (measures satisfaction); and *outcome* (includes definition and measurement of objectives, assessing the results and using them to improve later programmes). Others such as those of Parker (1976) and Jackson and Kulp (1979) evaluate participant reactions and knowledge gained, as well as knowledge and skill application and its effects on group and organizational performance. The evaluation models of Holton (1996) and Kraiger (2002) also include a number of individual and work environment characteristics known to influence learning transfer, which were discussed in earlier chapters but will not receive attention in this one as the focus here is on measurement of learning and transfer outcomes.

### THE KIRKPATRICK FRAMEWORK

Although it contains many of the same elements as frameworks already described, the most enduring seems to be that of Kirkpatrick (1977; 1979). As such it will be discussed in a little more detail here. Kirkpatrick proposed a taxonomy of outcomes at four levels – reactions, learning, behaviour and organizational impact. These will be described briefly.

*Participant reactions to the event*   Evaluation at this level measures how well trainees liked a particular programme, and in many respects is really no more than a measure of 'customer satisfaction'. At this level, trainers are interested in the answers to questions concerning the subject matter, training techniques, performance of the course leader, suggestions for improvement and so on. Despite their shortcomings (they are limited in scope, lack links with learning transfer and are often used as the only indication of effectiveness for many programmes), reactions evaluations will at the very least give an indication of what is 'going down well' or otherwise. Having said that, it would appear that answers to questions focusing on the usefulness or otherwise of the programme (utility reactions) have a stronger relationship with subsequent job performance than other reactions questions. Reactions evaluations can also be used to ascertain specific views concerning pace, depth and breadth of content, and teaching and facilitating styles, as well as practical matters such as timing, programme support or even choice of venue.

*The amount of learning that has taken place*   Getting a favourable reaction to a particular programme does not however ensure that learning will take place (learning can sometimes be painful!). Learning from a programme can take many forms, involving changes in knowledge, skills or attitudes. Different learning outcomes may happen simultaneously, sometimes resulting in a change in behaviour, sometimes not.

*Changes in behaviour at work, or learning transfer*   For most organizational learning interventions, in practical terms this is the outcome they want to achieve. We will see, through the work of Alliger and others, summarized below, that there are some links between measures of learning and of transfer in some studies. However they also show us that these links cannot be relied on, as measurement at every level has its own purpose. In evaluating the amount of learning transfer, we're trying to find out the extent to which learning from an intervention is being applied in practice. We want to know if managers are running their meetings better, frontline staff are treating their customers better, or salespeople are closing sales better. We'll come back to this later in the chapter.

*Measuring organizational impact*   This is usually the most difficult to measure, due to complication by other factors. As such it is rarely attempted in any meaningful way by most organizations. The primary difficulty they encounter is in determining how much of the improvement is due to the training as compared to other factors such as management style, staff morale or favourable economic conditions. This type of evaluation often compares figures before and after such as productivity, accident rates, absenteeism, sales figures or cost savings.

## Where to Start?

So, what level of measurement is appropriate, given the challenges outlined above? It seems that organizations generally seek to evaluate their training and development programmes for one or both of the following reasons. On one hand, they may want to prove (or at least provide evidence) that the programme has had an impact on some aspect of organizational performance, such as increasing productivity, improving service delivery or lowering the level of absenteeism. Evaluations of this nature usually look for relationships between aspects of the programme such as knowledge gained or behaviour changed and relevant organizational measures. Measurements of this kind are often what top managers want to see, as they give a clear indication (if measured reliably of course) of the effect of a learning intervention. On the other hand, evaluations may want to focus on improving both the content and delivery of future programmes. In these cases, emphasis needs to be put on the content and delivery of the programmes themselves, as well as other factors contributing to learning and application of that learning.

The work of Alliger and colleagues (Alliger and Janak 1989; Alliger et al. 1997) provides a useful starting point. Reporting on the widespread use of the Kirkpatrick framework, their earlier meta-analysis (an analysis of studies already undertaken) and later update came up with some interesting propositions. Generally speaking:

- outcomes at the reactions level are unrelated to those at other levels;

- outcomes at the learning level are no better predictors of subsequent job performance than utility reactions;

- whilst some correlations between outcomes at behaviour levels and organizational impact levels have been observed, they are influenced by many variables.

## Measurement at Different Levels

The main implication from the above is that evaluation at each level has its own purpose. Given what has been said, evaluation at the level of reactions is very easy to do, but provides information that is of limited use. At the other end of the spectrum, measurement of the contribution of training and development to overall organizational performance, particularly to the degree where a return on investment (Phillips 2003) can be calculated is seen by many as the ultimate goal for organizations, and the main reason they allocate precious resources to training and development. Realistically however, evaluation at this level is notoriously difficult to do validly and reliably. It can be time-consuming and therefore expensive, and in the case of shorter interventions could cost as much as the intervention itself. Luckily for us, therefore, the focus of this chapter is on evaluation at the behavioural level, which is more straightforward, can be measured validly and reliably, and has the advantage of being able to be more closely linked to the intervention. In practice of course, evaluating at the behaviour level is about evaluating learning transfer.

## Other Learning Outcomes

Before we discuss evaluation of learning transfer, it should be pointed out that there is another level at which it is often appropriate to measure outcomes. Throughout this book, the emphasis has been on transfer of learning in the sense that participants at learning events demonstrate changed behaviours at some stage after their return to the workplace. Yet it's not at all uncommon to hear people who have attended such an event to suggest upon their return that although they enjoyed it and/or found it useful, they didn't necessarily feel they learned anything new. For specific skills programmes, this may be slightly unfortunate, but not necessarily a big problem. However, for more and more programmes, such as management development interventions, where the emphasis may be on reinforcing good practice, building a new team, or generating new ways of dealing with problems, these types of outcome are perfectly valid.

## Alpha, Beta and Gamma Change

One approach to discussion of the multi-faceted nature of learning outcomes is that originally put forward by Golembiewski, Billingsley and Jaeger (1976). They highlighted the complexity of change in many learning interventions, and explain it by proposing three types of change that can occur – alpha, beta and gamma change. These will now be discussed.

---

**BOX 7.1: A VARIETY OF LEARNING OUTCOMES**

Teresa works in the accident and emergency unit of a mid-sized regional hospital, managing a 10-strong team of nurses and assistants. As part of a drive to improve the management capability of people in her position, she has just attended a specially designed development programme. The programme, which had a strong action learning component, involved some 20 days of meeting in action learning sets and plenary sessions over a period of 12 months.

The programme had a number of effects on Teresa. Certainly, there were some areas in which she increased her knowledge. How to run more effective meetings was one. Understanding what goes into constructing a budget for the unit was another. Then there were some other changes which only became apparent over time. For instance, up to the time she started the programme she had always considered herself a good listener. However, the nature of the programme (it was run on a residential basis in 3-day blocks) gave all participants plenty of time to meet informally and, as relationships built up, be honest with each other. Feedback she received over time suggested she might have some shortcomings in this direction. This was particularly interesting when completing a questionnaire on competencies developed in the course of the programme – her pre-programme score was actually higher than her post-programme score, even though she knew she had learned some valuable lessons. It was only when she reflected back (she was chosen to be interviewed as part of a follow-up evaluation) that she recognized the changes that had taken place.

---

## ALPHA CHANGE

This type of change is described as a straightforward variation in the level of knowledge or skill on some dimension along a fixed scale. For a simple skills course, for example, it could reflect a measurable improvement in the performance of a task such as constructing a spreadsheet, making a travel reservation, or negotiating a better price for a product. For a management programme, alpha change might include improved time and priority management, more effective meetings, better handling of conflict or better skill in delegating.

## BETA CHANGE

Beta change can be described as involving some 'recalibration' of the measurement scale, for example where participants may have reassessed their level of prior knowledge on some dimension in between two measurements. For instance, an individual may feel, following a programme they attend, that they didn't learn anything new as such, but what they did learn was simply a reinforcement of what they felt they were doing all along. What may have happened for them is that their procedural skills and knowledge have been placed in a declarative context (procedural and declarative knowledge were discussed in Chapter 2), so they now have a framework into which they can place what they know. For another, the intervention might allow them the opportunity to take stock of their understanding of certain relevant competencies (how to manage performance, for example) which may change as the intervention progresses.

## GAMMA CHANGE

Finally, gamma change can be described in terms of involving a reconceptualization, or a major change in the frame of reference within which the learning takes place. Some examples of gamma change outcomes might include participants coming away from a programme with greater self-insight regarding their style, their strengths or weaknesses, or their development needs. Perhaps they have found a new degree of clarity around their role, or a general broadening of their horizons and what is possible within that role. These outcomes are not easy to measure, but are valid outcomes nonetheless. A summary of a set of possible alpha, beta and gamma outcomes from a management development programme is shown in Table 7.1.

## Evaluating Learning Transfer

All research methods have their strengths and their weaknesses. Administering a survey questionnaire to look for correlations between variables can be fast and efficient. However, as the literature indicates, transfer of learning can be a complex matter, and while correlations indicate relationships between elements, they don't help the evaluator to understand processes or individual meaning in those elements. With more descriptive research, on the other hand, these difficulties can be more easily overcome, although it is time-consuming, and analysis is often more difficult.

In practical terms, the use of more than one method in evaluation should help achieve the best of both worlds. Sometimes referred to as multi-method research or triangulation, the use of multiple and independent methods (usually complementary qualitative and quantitative methods) should, according to Gill and Johnson (1991), have greater validity and reliability than a single method approach, assuming the same conclusions are reached. By obtaining corroborating

**Table 7.1        Alpha, beta and gamma change in summary**

| Alpha change | Beta change | Gamma change |
| --- | --- | --- |
| More effective meetings | Reinforcement of what one is already doing | Self-insight into own capabilities, preferences, and areas for development |
| Dealing with conflict better | | |
| Greater delegation and empowerment | Understanding competency and what competency in different areas comprises | Clarity of role within the current organization |
| Better communication | Greater confidence in job performance | Opening of mind and broadening one's horizons, exposure to new ideas and ways of managing |
| Better performance management | A more strategic view of the job of managing | |
| Better time and priority management | | Affirming a new way of managing for self |
| Hidden learning, which may only become apparent later | | |

evidence from different evaluation methods, the tradeoffs that must be made in conducting any research (McGrath 1982) can be dealt with. Triangulation is a means of minimizing the negative effects of these compromises in research and is defined by Loveridge (1990) as using multiple methods to capture a sense of reality. While different types of triangulation exist (Denzin 1978), the gathering of data either from different sources or by using different methods are the most common. For example, using a survey questionnaire will facilitate speedy gathering of data from a large number of people, but sacrifices depth at the expense of breadth. In a complementary way, in-depth interviews can provide richness, and thus help provide a more complete picture of the outcomes to be measured. Interestingly, in a review of research strategies employed over the previous 20 years, Scandura and Williams (2000) seem concerned that the use of single-source data has been increasing during the 1990s and suggest a need for greater use of triangulation in order to strengthen the conclusions drawn and reduce threats to their validity. In fact, Patton (1990, 187) goes so far as to 'offer as a methodological rule the principle that multiple methods should be used in every investigation'.

## How to Measure Learning Transfer

As this book is not about evaluation in general, the emphasis in this chapter is more on the measurement of learning transfer. The choice of measure with which to evaluate the amount of learning transfer from an intervention is an important one. Evaluators must be clear about the purpose of the evaluation, being clear on the distinction between *proving* and *improving* as discussed earlier. If the emphasis is on proving, then 'hard' data, such as is gained from the scores on competency profiles or supervisor reports, will be what's more likely to be listened to. If, on the other hand, the evaluation has more to do with finding out why or how certain elements worked or didn't, or is about making the programme better for the future, then the sort of information gained from interviews, focus groups and other qualitative methods is likely to be of greater value.

Effective training begins with identifying a training need. This need is usually expressed in terms of knowledge, skills or attitudes (often referred to collectively as KSAs) which need to be learned or changed. The difference between the existing level of KSAs and the desired level can be called the performance gap. The objectives of a training event become the statement of how that event will close the gap and evaluation of the outcomes of the training will determine whether or not this has been achieved. In reality, therefore, it's at the analysis stage that the evaluation process actually begins. Indeed measures which are taken before a training event are often part of the training needs analysis process itself. Other measures may be taken during an event to see if the required changes are taking place and to allow modifications to the training to be made if necessary. Finally, measures may be taken after the event, at times ranging from immediately afterwards to a number of years later, in order to demonstrate if the performance gap has finally been narrowed.

## Response-shift Bias

Before moving on to discuss evaluation methods, it's worth saying a word or two about an issue that arises specifically with self-reporting measures, known as response-shift bias. Some research by Terborg, Howard and Maxwell (1980) reported a number of studies that showed that self-reports including pre- and post-ratings are subject to this phenomenon. It occurs when the actual training intervention changes the evaluation standard for the dimension being measured. The difficulty arises when the intervention (such as a development programme) changes the participant's evaluation standard for the dimension measured, in effect the beta change we discussed earlier in the chapter. It is more likely to occur in training and development interventions where outcomes other than the acquisition of straightforward knowledge or simple skills are involved. To take an example, a participant on a supervisory programme may rate himself pre-course as a 5 (out of 7, say) on the dimension of communication skills. As a result of attendance at the programme, his knowledge of what constitutes good communication skills expands. When asked to rate himself at the end of the programme, he now realizes his pre-course level of communication skill was really only a 3, and given what he has learned, he is now a 5. Ordinary pre- and post-training measures would conclude that the programme was ineffective. To get around this (and indeed to measure both alpha and beta change) Howard and Dailey (1979) recommend what is in effect a three-test approach. First, the normal pre-course level is rated. After the training, participants give two ratings: the first is the level they perceive themselves to be at currently (the usual post-course rating); the second rating is how they *now* perceive themselves to have been just before the training started. Howard and Dailey call this second measure the 'then' measure. The response-shift is the difference between the 'pre' and the 'then' measure, and indeed can be used as a measure of learning. The difference between the 'post' and 'then' measures represents the true (behaviour level) effect of the training.

Results from a number of studies bear this out. In five out of 11 studies carried out by Howard and others during 1979, analyses comparing pre/post and then/post measures showed very different conclusions, that is, different levels of improvement. More recent work by Sprangers and Hoogstraten (1989) and Mann (1997) lend support to the usefulness of this technique for evaluating different learning outcomes and giving a truer picture of the amount of change that has taken place.

## Evaluation Methods

With regard to evaluation at the behaviour (learning transfer) level, a number of (sometimes complementary) methods can be employed to do so. The principal ones are described below. Some of these can be applied during a programme, but in most cases need to be applied some time after the programme has been completed. The 'delay' is important for two reasons. Firstly, it is unreasonable in most cases to expect behaviour to change immediately as a result of attendance at a training event. Secondly, it is reasonable that evaluation of a training event will be more rational and considered at some distance from the event, when not caught up in the event itself.

We will now look at some of the most popular evaluation methods in use.

## QUESTIONNAIRES

Perhaps the most used (and in many cases overused) method of gathering data relating to learning transfer is the questionnaire. Critics argue that questionnaires, particularly where assessments of skill are concerned, are highly subjective. However, this can be reduced to some extent by asking the subject's boss, peers or subordinates to complete them – in effect a form of triangulation as discussed earlier. Another difficulty with questionnaires is that it is very difficult to construct them in a readily understandable, valid and reliable format. Nevertheless, they have become an extremely popular tool in the evaluation process. Questionnaires may be used in many forms for this purpose. Ranking scales, semantic differential questionnaires or Likert scales are common examples.

So, in terms of specific measurement of changes in behaviour, some of the questionnaire types outlined above, based on application outcomes, can be appropriate. For instance if a learning intervention has been designed in a systematic way, it should have a set of objectives that the intervention is designed to achieve. If those objectives can be described in application-oriented terms so much the better. Once these are clear, it becomes easier to see what specific skills, behaviours or competencies need to be exhibited by participants following the intervention, to demonstrate success. This is becoming increasingly important as more and more programmes, particularly in the area of management, are built around the development of a set of competencies to be acquired or desired behaviours to be demonstrated (Burke 1997; Warr, Allan and Birdi 1999). In these cases, measuring outcomes essentially becomes a relatively straightforward process of asking questions within the relevant competency areas, or about the desired behaviours.

An example should help. Let us say a management development programme within a large supermarket chain aims to promote better people management capability amongst its store managers, arguing (quite correctly) that better people management at store level translates 'across the counter' into increased customer satisfaction and loyalty and thus better bottom-line performance for the store. Thus the 'managing individual performance' scale might include behaviours like the following to be demonstrated:

- delegates appropriate tasks, and allows the individual to get on with them;

- regularly reviews with individuals their progress towards achieving goals;

- gives clear and honest feedback regarding an individual's strengths and weaknesses.

If behaviours are stated in this way, it is a very simple step to convert this into a questionnaire, perhaps in the form of a Likert-type scale with say five to seven options, ranging from strongly disagree to strongly agree. There are two sets of benefits for measuring learning transfer in this way, and indeed they incorporate the twin objectives of proving and improving that were discussed earlier. Ongoing measurement of the changes in behaviour (for example every 6 months or a year) will provide an organizational indication of the improvement or otherwise in the standard of people management throughout the organization. The more data that is available, the more generalizations can be made, or the more comparisons can be made between departments, periods in time, and so on. However it is arguable that an even larger benefit can accrue from focusing on the individual level. Data from such a profile can serve as a very important starting point for improvement and development. Conversations around maintenance of strengths and concentration on appropriate areas for development can take place, while at the same time having comparative evidence with which to gauge progress.

There's no doubt that 'hard' data from questionnaire responses is satisfying for those who like such things. However, while data from questionnaires can tell you 'what', they're not very good for answering 'how' or 'why' questions relating to learning transfer. For instance, you may find out that managers in the finance department have moved up a half-point on average in terms of how good they are at giving feedback, but you still don't know what could be done to make that improvement even greater. In these circumstances, the use of additional techniques such as interviews or focus groups will be more likely to provide those answers.

## INTERVIEWS

If time and resources allow, a properly structured and conducted interview can glean a large amount of rich data concerning learning transfer. In the same way as responses to questionnaires are good for answering the 'what' questions, data gathered through interviews can be extremely useful in answering the 'how' questions. How they are used will depend to an extent on whether the

---

**BOX 7.2: EVALUATION AT THE BEHAVIOUR LEVEL**

A large international hotel group, with properties in several European countries, recently completed a 5-day leadership programme for its senior levels of management, some 200 people in all. Based around a set of eight core leadership competencies, the programme featured inputs, cases, discussions and projects designed to improve managers' capabilities on those competencies, seen as essential for leadership of the group into the future. A 40-item instrument capturing examples of the competencies in action, and that could be used on a 360 degree basis, was specially designed. Before attending the programme, participants were required to self-assess on the competencies, and to have the questionnaires completed by their direct reports. Analysis of the results was handled externally. During the course of the programme, results from completion of the questionnaires were fed back to participants on an individual basis, with coaching sessions built in to facilitate understanding of the data. As well as providing a focus for programme content, individuals' competency profiles and their implications acted as an important input to their action plans, which were completed on the final day.

Six months after the programme, during which time participants had attended a follow-up day to review progress on action plans and had received further support in the form of coaching, competency profiles were again constructed in the same way as before, using self-assessment and responses from direct reports. On an individual basis, participants were clearly able to see on what dimensions they had changed (if at all) and compare achievements with their action plans. At a broader level, analysis of the overall data enabled top management to compare highs, lows and priorities for the future across ranks and regions, and to provide a starting point for identification of organizational barriers to learning transfer.

---

emphasis is on describing events or explaining them. On the one hand, there may be a need to describe the relevant behaviours, attitudes and events in force during the process of learning transfer. In this situation, a more structured interview may be called for. On the other hand, it may be necessary to explain the process in detail, looking at the range of factors influencing transfer, and identifying possible causes and consequences. In this situation, a less structured interview may be a better option. The structured form tends to take up less time, is easier to conduct for the less experienced interviewer, and, as the questions are usually predetermined, can obtain the desired information. However, if the format is too structured, below-the-surface issues may be ignored. The unstructured interview, by contrast, requires greater skill on the part of the interviewer, but can be more powerful at gaining richer information

(Denzin 1970) such as perceptions, feelings or attitudes. In practice, given that sometimes both emphases will be needed, a semi-structured format (Easterby-Smith, Thorpe and Lowe 1991; Remenyi et al. 1998) with an interview guide is regularly used. The guide helps to provide some structure, and helps to provide consistency if data is being collected from a number of different sites. This facilitates the making of comparisons during analysis.

## FOCUS GROUPS

So far we have seen that questionnaires can help gather data quickly, and provide 'hard' data, but that such data can often suffer from a lack of depth. Alternatively, while interviews can provide this depth, the time and cost involved in gathering sufficient views to make the data reliable can be off-putting. For many evaluators, therefore, the use of the focus group has been seen as providing a reasonable trade-off between these two aims. Focus group meetings are a popular means of gathering evidence for learning transfer. Assuming they are used in the right way, they can also be quite effective.

At the start of a process, they can be used where the objective is to gather views in a general way, and to get a sense of themes that might be emerging. For example, many consultants and researchers use focus groups in just this way to identify themes around which they can design a survey questionnaire for future evaluations. At the other end of the process, they can be particularly useful for providing depth to a more quantitative survey. For instance, a survey administered following a programme might ask questions concerning the level of management support participants experienced in putting their learning into practice. Suppose overall average scores are in the medium range, and survey results also indicate a wide variation in scores on this dimension. Further analysis of these results via a focus group would be able to get behind both the high and the low scores, providing greater explanation as to how and why some participants' managers are very good and others very poor at giving support. In this way, what good and bad management support actually looks like could be identified. Data of this nature can be far more useful in making plans to improve learning transfer from future programmes.

## OBSERVATION

Observing participants to record changes in their behaviour provides immediate feedback regarding skill application. This technique is in regular use in the teaching of skills such as presenting, interviewing, negotiating and customer handling, to name but a few, and for these types of skills it can be both valid and reliable. It can also be used before, within or after a training event. Used before and after training events, it can provide a clear picture of pre- and post-training performance, and enable comparison. Used within training events, feedback from the observer(s) can guide practice and enable mastery of the skill. For data gathered through this method to be valid and reliable it needs to be clear what specific behaviours are being observed, and what the 'correct' behaviour is. Of course best results will be obtained if the people doing the observing are skilled in doing so. They need mastery of the skill in which the training is being conducted (procedural knowledge), as well as a sound knowledge of the principles behind it (declarative knowledge). In reality, however, this is not always practically possible. In those situations, some others in the training group may be given guidelines and asked to observe. While this form of observation is not quite as valid, it is nevertheless usually more achievable. Also, where more than one observer is involved, shortcomings arising from a lack of depth in their collective knowledge of the subject can be offset by the number of viewpoints they can provide. This may not be a major issue during the training, as observers will usually have the backup of the facilitator. However if follow-up observations are to be made back at work, care must be taken as to who carries them out. The provision of a clear template and set of guidelines for the observer will help with the accuracy of data collected in this way.

Technology can also help. The (small) size and relatively small cost of a variety of devices with which observations can be made continues to make the process easier. Performance on a presentation skills course, for example, or difficulties encountered in chairing a meeting can be recorded unobtrusively using audio or (better still) video equipment. What these instruments capture can strongly reinforce observations made by an observer. In addition, they are not subject to any biases, and have the benefit of being able to be retained for further reflection.

## EXAMINATION OF ACTION PLANS

Although not in itself an evaluation method, we saw in Chapter 3 that having a specific plan to put into practice skills or knowledge gained from a training or development event will increase the possibility of their transfer to the job. The value of stating objectives in the action plan as specifically and measurably as possible (remember SMART?) will be realized when it comes to measurement of their achievement or otherwise. Actual changes in on-the-job behaviour (learning transfer) can be compared with predicted changes as described in the action plan. The value of this process can be further enhanced if the individual includes, while creating the action plan, a reflection on their current capabilities in the area of competence being developed. Changes can be measured by interview, by questionnaire, or indeed by any appropriate means at a specified date following the event.

## SELF DIARIES

Before training, self diaries can provide a baseline measure of efficiency or effectiveness on some dimension. Maintaining a self diary involves recording actions, decisions and other activities at work for a specific period of time. The same process is then followed under the same conditions following the training. Evaluation becomes the measurement of the difference between the two. For example, a self diary could be useful for evaluating the effectiveness of a time management course. A typical morning's entries could include the number of and time spent on phone calls, the number of interruptions, by whom, how much time was spent on identified key result areas, and so on. However, the use of self diaries does rely heavily on the commitment and honesty of the person completing them.

## CRITICAL INCIDENTS

Not unlike the diary approach, but for specific incidents, this requires the trainee to describe in detail a particular work-related incident of relevance to the training. How they behaved, decisions they took and so on are recorded. Quite apart from any evaluative need, these descriptions can serve as useful inputs to the training process, given that they encourage reflection. After the training, similar incidents (when they arise) can be described and different behaviours noted and discussed. The technique could be used for example to evaluate the outcomes of a negotiating skills course, in which the participant describes matters such as their feelings before a particular negotiation session, how they planned it, what strategies they used during it, what the outcome was, and so on.

## Other Sources of Data

In many evaluation studies over the years, a variety of the methods described above have been used. Trainees have been interviewed before, during and after programmes, completed questionnaires and been asked about current behaviour, critical incidents, intentions, attitudes and values (Bennett, Lehman and Forst 1999; Clarke 2002). In these studies, the focus has tended to be on reports from the trainees themselves. However, in an increasing number of evaluation studies, others such as peers, managers, direct reports or customers are asked to provide evidence of learning transfer. Thus the use of instruments that gather information from sources other than trainees is increasing. Gaining steadily in popularity amongst the management community are instruments such as 360 degree-type feedback instruments. Conger and Xin (2000), for example, found in a survey of executive education that 76 per cent of respondents felt that such instruments would be used extensively in the 21st century, particularly in the area of behaviour change and outcomes linked to programme objectives. That's heartening. So too are a recent review and a study, by Alliger et al. (1997) and May and Kahnweiler (2000) respectively, that support this development. However, great care must be taken with the use of these instruments. Atkins and Wood (2002) describe research into the validity of 360-degree feedback with some external criteria. Their results add to the evidence that self-ratings tend to be more lenient than those of observers such as peers or supervisors, and that ratings by observers agree more with each other than with the self-rating. They also warn that mixing self- and others' ratings is not a good idea from the point of view of providing an accurate picture. All of this makes sense. Different people will view an individual's performance from different angles, and indeed it is the diversity of these viewpoints that makes the data they generate so valuable. Finally, there is a logistical difficulty that can arise when trying to generate reports from more than one source. Before-and-after measures of on-the-job behaviour are valid and reliable measures of transfer where respondents have been able to experience or observe that behaviour on a regular basis. However, generating sufficient reports to make them so can sometimes be a problem, as can finding programmes that measure behaviours or competencies in this way. Despite these potential problems, gathering data through this multi-source mode offers an additional means of triangulating to that discussed earlier, that of gathering data from the same sources, but using different methods.

## Control Groups

Another very important consideration when evaluating any training intervention is the use of control groups. These are essential if changes in behaviour resulting from the training are to be isolated and attributed solely to the training. It is often the case, particularly with lengthy development-type programmes, that learning or change in behaviour can occur independently of the training being attended. Measurement of changes in the dimensions being studied in a group which is matched in terms of appropriate characteristics to the experimental group, and which has not undergone the training, will allow the researcher to determine with greater validity the actual effect of the training. A more sophisticated approach than the Howard and Dailey model is a scientific approach originally proposed way back by Solomon, (1949). This approach uses three control groups in addition to the experimental group. He suggests that due to the Hawthorne effect (a positive effect on the performance of a group brought about by paying special attention to that group), a control group may perform better on the after-training test as a result of having undergone the before-training test. Therefore, in his 'four-group design' one control group receives before-and-after testing and no training, one receives before-and-after testing and a training placebo, and one receives after-training testing only. However, the practical difficulties in trying to carry out this type of evaluation in practice are enormous. Nevertheless, Kirkpatrick, (1977) and others argue for the necessity of control groups to provide proof, rather than evidence, of change.

Perhaps the value of rigorous evaluation of the benefits (or otherwise) of training, whatever the methodology used, is best summed up in Kirkpatrick's own words (Kirkpatrick 1977, 12):

> *Learn all you can about evaluation. Next, gather evidence that your programs are effective. If they are not, don't broadcast the evidence. Just work at improving your programs so that the evidence will be positive and then communicate it to your superiors. Most superiors will be most happy and will not ask for proof. However, as time and money permit, gather proof of the effectiveness of your programs. And if the proof shows an effective program, broadcast it around the world.*

## In Practice

What follows is an extract from two evaluation projects that were carried out in two different organizational settings. The first was a survey of all the learning and development interventions undertaken for managerial and administrative staff in a medium-sized (250 employees) manufacturing organization. Interventions included workshops, short skills courses, longer development programmes, conferences and seminars, and ranged in length from half a day to 25 days. Although evaluation at all levels was included, there was specific interest in evaluation at the behaviour (learning transfer) level, given its links with the impact on the organization, and the difficulty in measuring the latter. The second evaluation project was carried out on behalf of a small management training consultancy that wished to get a sense of the degree of behaviour change by customers on its courses and workshops. Interventions in this case included sales management courses, finance workshops, personal development workshops and a development programme for small business owners. Results from the first study reinforce the importance of triangulating (in this case getting data from more than one source using more than one method), particularly in the absence of baseline data, while the second illustrates the range of outcomes that can be measured, even if no baseline measures are available. Both also demonstrate the importance of other factors discussed in earlier chapters, particularly those around motivation to learn and to transfer.

## EVALUATION STUDY 1

Information was gathered via focus groups and some individual interviews. In addition, the Learning Transfer Evaluation (LTE) instrument measured perceptions of training programme and workplace factors known to affect learning transfer. None of the courses delivered was based around any set of behavioural or competency measures that could be measured pre- and post-course, so measurement of changes in behaviour resulting from training were necessarily subjective. Comments such as 'small things stick in your mind', or 'you'd be aware for a while' were common. At no stage did any individual suggest that any course they attended hadn't at least 'given them something to think about'. LTE results regarding participants' perceptions of learning were also of interest. The average score from 37 respondents (few of whom attended focus groups) was a respectable 3.43 (on a scale of 1–5), with scores ranging from 2.20 to 4.00. This underlined the wide variation in learning experienced and supported the 'hit and miss' nature of the organization's training and development efforts. In general, however, perceptions of learning were reasonably high. Additionally, the overall score from the LTE for participants' motivation to transfer was 3.78 and generally consistent, suggesting that participants had reasonable intentions of applying what they learned on their return to work.

Notwithstanding the subjective nature of participant perceptions regarding learning and application, it was decided to ask attendees at focus groups to rate, also on a scale of 1 to 5, their perception of the amount of behaviour change resulting from their attendance at a particular course. Twenty-five attendees reported an average change of only 1.6 in the score. This was considered a small change, particularly given a tendency for respondents to overestimate rather than underestimate, and despite the positive scores for learning and motivation to transfer. Furthermore, few participants were able to be specific in terms of what they were now doing differently back at work as a result of attending the training, suggesting that the learning reported didn't actually translate into changed behaviour back at work. Further discussion around the scores with the focus groups revealed that the scores depended greatly on perceptions of the relevance of the course they attended in the first place, and the presence or absence of support for application of learning back at work. This information was able to form the basis of a number of recommendations for improvement.

## EVALUATION STUDY 2

For this study, nine of the provider's programmes were chosen, and evaluated at different levels of the Kirkpatrick framework. Data concerning the extent to which participants applied their learning back at work (level 3) were collected in two ways. For some multi-module programmes, assignments had been given between modules, and participants asked to report, by means of describing critical incidents, the results of their efforts to put their action plan into effect. For two particular programmes, participants were asked in the course of a semi-structured interview to describe specifically ways in which their learning from the programme was being applied. They were asked *What are you doing differently in your business as a result of attending the programme?* As the construction of a strategic/business plan for their business was a requirement for both programmes, what most participants said they were now doing differently was using that strategic plan to guide their actions – in effect, implementing the plan. The following specific observations were reported (some of them several times) and attributed directly to attendance at the appropriate programme.

- Doing less 'operating' and more 'managing' – ranging from 30 per cent managing (before) to 95 per cent managing (after).

- Setting targets based on better-quality data – enabling greater certainty concerning the outcome.

- Improved focus on processes rather than ad-hoc decision making – including processes for health and safety (monitoring) and HR (regular performance reviews).

- Significantly improved work/life balance – such as a reduction in the working week of 15 hours in one case.

- Longer-term, more strategic planning – together with better monitoring, allowing more time and space to make adjustments.

- A new focus on profitable customers, having made key, evidence-based decisions regarding the dropping of unprofitable ones.

- More strategic involvement of staff in the business – leading to better decision making.

- A much clearer view of the cost of sales – enabling more accurate estimates of cost/profit.

- Overall, a greater confidence in developing the business for the future – gained from the support of other programme attendees and mentors.

Although the data above are subjective, the fact that they arose from discussion of specific critical incidents lends them a greater degree of credibility. This technique was chosen in particular to overcome deficiencies in participants' recall of what they actually learned and provide backup evidence for their claims regarding learning transfer.

## Summary

This chapter dealt with some frameworks and a variety of techniques that can be used to measure the amount of learning (alpha, beta and gamma change) and transfer resulting from a training or development intervention. Learning transfer is a distinct outcome, and although influenced by many other factors, provides valuable information concerning the effectiveness or otherwise of that intervention. The relative advantages of different qualitative and quantitative methods were discussed, and some important methodology issues (response-shift bias, triangulation and the use of control groups) highlighted.

## References

Alliger, G.M. and Janak, E.A. (1989). Kirkpatrick's levels of training criteria: Thirty years later. *Personnel Psychology*, 42, 331–41.

Alliger, G.M., Tannenbaum, S.I., Bennett W. Jr., Traver, H. and Shotland, A. (1997). A meta-analysis of the relations among training criteria. *Personnel Psychology*, 50(2), 341–58.

Atkins, P.W.B. and Wood, R.E. (2002). Self-versus others' ratings as predictors of assessment center ratings: Validation evidence for 360-degree feedback programs. *Personnel Psychology*, 55(4), 871–904.

Bennett, J.B., Lehman, W.E.K. and Forst, J.K. (1999). Change, transfer climate and customer orientation: A contextual model and analysis of change-driven training. *Group and Organization Management*, 24, 188–216.

Burke, L.A. (1997). Improving positive transfer: A test of relapse prevention training on transfer outcomes. *Human Resource Development Quarterly*, 8(2), 115–28.

Clarke, N. (2002). Job/work environment factors influencing training transfer within a human service agency: Some indicative support for Baldwin and Ford's transfer climate construct. *International Journal of Training and Development*, 6(3), 146–62.

Conger, J.A. and Xin, K. (2000). Executive education in the 21st century. *Journal of Management Education*, 24(1), 73–101.

Denzin, N.K. (1970). The Research Act in Sociology. London: Butterworth. In D. Silverman, Interpreting Qualitative Data: Methods for Analysing Talk, Text and Interaction. 2nd ed. London: Sage.

Denzin, N.K. (1978). *Sociological methods: A sourcebook.* New York: McGraw Hill.

Easterby-Smith, M., Thorpe, R. and Lowe, A. (1991). *Management research: An introduction.* London: Sage.

Gill, J. and Johnson, P. (1991). *Research methods for managers.* London: Paul Chapman Publishing Ltd.

Golembiewski, R.T., Billingsley, K. and Jaeger, S. (1976). Measuring change and persistence in human affairs. *Journal of Applied Behavioral Science*, 12, 133–57.

Holton, E.F. III. (1996). The flawed four level evaluation model. *Human Resource Development Quarterly*, 7, 5–21.

Howard, G.S. and Dailey, P.R. (1979). Response-shift bias: A source of contamination of self-report measures. *Journal of Applied Psychology*, 64, 144–50.

Jackson, S. and Kulp, M.J. (1979). Designing guidelines for evaluating the outcomes of management training. In J.J. Phillips, *Handbook of training and evaluation methods.* New York: Gulf Publishing Co.

Kirkpatrick, D.L. (1977). Evaluating training programs: Evidence vs proof. *Training and Development Journal*, 31(11), 8–12.

Kirkpatrick, D.L. (1979). Techniques for evaluating training programs. *Training and Development Journal*, 33(6), 78–92.

Kraiger, K. (2002). Decision-based evaluation. In K. Kraiger (ed.), *Creating, implementing, and managing effective training and development: State-of-the-art lessons for practice*. San Francisco: Jossey-Bass.

Loveridge, R. (1990). Triangulation – or how to survive your choice of business school PhD course. *Graduate Management Research*, 5(3), 18–25.

Mann, S. (1997). Implications of the response-shift bias for management. *Journal of Management Development*, 16, 328–37.

May, G.L. and Kahnweiler, W.M. (2000). The effect of a mastery practice design on learning and transfer in behaviour modelling training. *Personnel Psychology*, 53, 353–73.

McGrath, J.E. (1982). Dilemmatics: The study of research choices and dilemmas. In J.E. McGrath, J. Martin, and R.A. Kulka (eds.), *Judgement calls in research*. Beverly Hills, CA: Sage.

Parker, T.C. (1976). Statistical methods for measuring training results. In R.L. Craig (ed.), *Training and Development Handbook*. New York: McGraw Hill.

Patton, M.Q. (1990). *Qualitative evaluation and research methods. 2nd ed.* Newbury Park, CA: Sage.

Phillips, J.J. (2003). *Return on investment in training and performance improvement programs. 2nd ed.* Burlington, MA: Butterworth-Heinemann.

Remenyi, D., Williams, B., Money, A. and Swartz, E. (1998). *Doing research in business and management: An introduction to process and method*. London: Sage.

Scandura, T.A. and Williams, E.A. (2000). Research methodology in management: Current practices, trends, and implications for future research. *Academy of Management Journal*, 43(6), 1248–64.

Solomon, R.L. (1949). An extension of control group design. *Psychological Bulletin*, 46, 137–50.

Sprangers, M. and Hoogstraten, J. (1989). Pretesting effects in retrospective pre-test-post-test designs. *Journal of Applied Psychology*, 74(2), 265–72.

Terborg, J.R., Howard, G.S. and Maxwell, S.E. (1980). Evaluating planned organizational change: A method for assessing alpha, beta, and gamma change. *Academy of Management Review*, 5(1), 109–21.

Warr, P.B., Allan, C. and Birdi, K. (1999). Predicting three levels of training outcome. *Journal of Occupational and Organizational Psychology*, 72, 351–76.

Warr, P. Bird, M. and Rackham, N. (1970). *Evaluation of management training*. London: Gower Press.

# 8

# How to Improve Learning Transfer

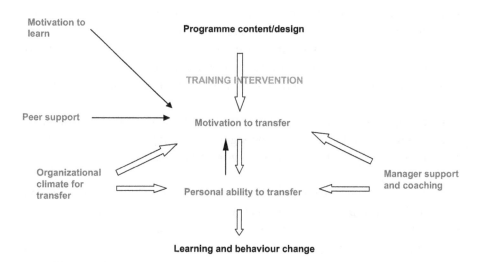

## Introduction

The purpose of this final chapter is to pull together the different strands that have been explored throughout the book, and to point the way towards improvement of learning transfer in the organization(s) with which you work. At the beginning of the book we saw that estimates of the amount of learning transfer – real changes in behaviour back at work – that takes place following learning interventions are on the whole quite low. We then went on to deal in detail with the different categories of factors that help or hinder learning transfer. These factors include characteristics of the learners themselves, characteristics of the learning interventions and characteristics of the work environments from which they come and to which they return following the intervention. We looked at how these factors can combine to help or hinder learning transfer efforts, by creating motivation and opportunity to apply learning, as well as potential areas of resistance. Finally, we suggested some straightforward techniques that can be applied to evaluate learning transfer.

## The Importance of Measurement

To pick up on the last point, the mere act of measuring the amount of learning transfer that has or has not taken place will not ensure that it will take place. But it is a critical starting point for improvement. Understanding what learning transfer has taken place and how it has done so will provide a clear indication of what needs to be done to ensure that it is maintained. Given what we've seen in previous chapters, a wide range of factors, captured in the learning transfer model in Chapter 1, will need to be taken into account. For example, if results from evaluation of a particular customer service initiative suggest that relatively little of the effort put into the initiative has resulted in real changes in customer service behaviour, the answers may come from a variety of sources. Perhaps the workshops that participants attended concentrated too much on theory and not enough on practice. Perhaps participants had no choice as to whether to attend the workshops, regardless of their current level of skill. Perhaps some participants don't deal with customers with any degree of regularity. Or perhaps they work for an old style manager who didn't give them any support or encouragement in trying out their new-found skills.

Therefore, getting a reading of the strength of these factors is an important starting point for improvement and is every bit as important as evaluation of the reactions, learning, behaviour change and organizational impact of any intervention. In this regard it is critically important to look at the whole learning system. In doing so the factors that have been described in earlier chapters as having an effect on learning transfer will need to be included. In summary, they are:

- participants' motivation to learn;

- the content and design of interventions;

- the effects of support from participants' peers and managers;

- the organizational climate for transfer;

- participants' motivation and ability to transfer learning back to the workplace;

- other learning outcomes that might be appropriate.

## Measurement Approaches

In Chapter 7, we described a number of methods that can be used to evaluate the results of learning and development efforts. We also saw that there are choices to be made between the more quantitative methods (such as the use of questionnaires), which can be fast and efficient, and the more qualitative methods (focus groups or interviews, for example) which help deepen our understanding. To get around the constraints posed by each of these approaches, the use of triangulation, gathering data from more than one source or by using different methods, was suggested.

In designing an effective learning transfer improvement project, these considerations are important. Data on some factors will be easier to get than on others, and so the purpose for which they are required will need to be clear. How the strength of the factors will be measured is another consideration. In using the data to make improvements to the learning transfer system, the possible pitfalls and likely sources of resistance is yet another. Finally, the results of the efforts should be evaluated and adjustments made where necessary. Thus a number of phases will need to be tackled in turn – diagnosis, implementation and evaluation.

## The Diagnostic Phase

A diagnosis of the state of learning transfer in an organization is usually undertaken for one of two reasons. It may be undertaken for a specific purpose, to determine what factors contributed to the degree of learning transfer of a particular intervention. It may also be undertaken in a more general sense, where the focus is less on particular interventions and more on the conditions in the workplace that help or hinder application of learning. In either case, the same factors should be examined, although the emphasis may differ somewhat.

### PARTICIPANT MOTIVATION TO LEARN

We saw in Chapter 5 the main factors that affect participants' motivation to take on and learn from a programme. These include their expectancies surrounding the programme, their job and career attitudes, their locus of control, their goal orientation and in particular their self-efficacy, or level of confidence in their ability to make the programme work for them. In practice, it may not be possible to measure the effects of some of these factors, as by and large they represent personal characteristics, and as such are not susceptible to any meaningful change. However, the coaching role of the manager, identified as an important contributor to the creation of a learning climate, can be important here. One of the most important functions of a manager as coach is to create conditions where people can give of their best. In enabling this, managers need to understand their people and the way they approach their work. Therefore, understanding their attitude to work, how they attribute success or failure, and the way they approach the performance of their job will all provide information about how they might respond to and benefit from different learning initiatives.

## THE CONTENT AND DESIGN OF INTERVENTIONS

With regard to learning interventions themselves, Chapter 2 identified a large number of components of an effective intervention, and described how each of them can positively influence learning transfer. Therefore, examination of proposed learning interventions with regard to the presence or absence of these elements is critical. For example, is an intervention a response to a validly and reliably identified need? Are the objectives of the intervention clear and appropriate? In terms of the content, does it balance declarative and procedural knowledge? In terms of the design, does it use adult learning principles? Is sufficient time allowed for practice? There are many other considerations, discussed in Chapter 2, which can form the basis of the examination.

Post-programme, what follow up support activities have been considered? Will participants be asked to create a specific and measurable action plan? Is coaching, whether provided in-house or by an external coach, a feature? These 'maintenance of behaviour' activities involving goal setting and self-management (discussed in Chapter 3) have been shown to facilitate learning transfer and as such should be included in the diagnosis.

## PEER, MANAGER AND ORGANIZATIONAL SUPPORT

The effects of support (or otherwise) from peers, the organization in general and line managers in particular were dealt with in Chapter 4. As with other factors already discussed, these can have significant effects on learning transfer and need to be included. While the influence of peer and organizational support can vary greatly from one work environment to another, the importance of manager support and coaching cannot be underestimated. Therefore measurement of its effect should be central to the review. In particular, issues such as the amount of coaching and feedback received and the level of openness to new ideas in the work unit are significant influencing factors.

It is probably at this stage that account needs to be taken of the level of support or resistance in the broader organization that might have an influence. Chapter 6 looked at some possible sources and types of resistance that work against learning transfer efforts. While they are unlikely to be strong determinants of the degree to which transfer will be facilitated, they should at least be considered.

## PARTICIPANTS' MOTIVATION AND ABILITY TO TRANSFER

The assessment of individuals' motivation and ability to transfer are two critical elements in improving learning transfer, with the latter being the means by which the former becomes a reality. They are also the factors likely to correlate most significantly with actual transfer. We saw in Chapter 5 how this works, and how both factors can be influenced by individual, training design and work environment characteristics. Thus evidence for the degree of motivation to transfer as well as the amount of time and mental space available to do so should be available through examination of these characteristics.

## OTHER LEARNING OUTCOMES

Finally, it may also be appropriate to determine if learning outcomes other than those expected have emerged from previous interventions. Their presence may reveal hitherto hidden benefits which, now in the open, can be used to positive effect in the future. Learning outcomes were discussed in Chapter 7.

## CONDUCTING THE DIAGNOSIS

As suggested at the beginning of this chapter, there are choices to be made regarding how the conditions for learning transfer will be diagnosed – essentially through a quantitative approach, a qualitative approach, or a combination of both. The benefits of using both approaches to offset the shortcomings of either have already been discussed, and can provide depth as well as breadth to the results.

If large numbers of participants are involved, or the information is to be used primarily to get a sense of the main themes for later exploration, the analyst will need to find an instrument that captures data on relevant factors. Within the research community, many researchers have developed their own instruments, usually for use in specific research settings. For more general use, this author has developed the Learning Transfer Evaluation (LTE), a 48-item instrument that measures the strength of eight factors (all of which can be changed) known to affect learning transfer. It may of course be appropriate to develop one's own instrument.

Scores on a questionnaire will give a good overall picture. However, if really rich data is required, or indeed if the numbers involved in the programme are small, then a more qualitative approach is indicated. Conducting a semi-structured interview with a sample of participants can be very valuable in getting to understand how the learning transfer process has worked, and where the major issues are. Questions can be asked around the factors considered important, and perceptions gathered concerning their effects. As a starter, Table 8.1 provides a possible set of opening questions for conducting these interviews. These questions can form the basis of an in-depth interview which would yield rich data and point the way towards what needs to be done to improve conditions for learning transfer.

A further option which is quite common in diagnosis is the use of a focus group. Focus groups can explore issues more deeply than survey questionnaires, although they don't usually permit the same depth of analysis as would an interview. Nevertheless, they can be very useful, particularly when used in conjunction with a more quantitative instrument. For example, a focus group discussion could be used initially to raise issues of importance to learning transfer, which could then form the basis of a broader survey. On the other hand, issues raised in a survey could be explored in more depth with a focus group. In either case, the questions outlined in Table 8.1 could form the basis of that discussion.

## ANALYSIS OF THE DATA

Once gathered, the data needs to be analyzed. This may be quite a straightforward matter, with the major areas for attention featuring quite prominently in the responses. Or it may take a little more effort, comparing evidence from one source with evidence from another, investigating inconsistencies and refining understanding. In any event, the output of the analysis should give rise to a clear set of priorities to be addressed in order to improve conditions for learning transfer.

## The Implementation Phase

This phase concerns itself with applying what is known about influences on learning transfer to make it easier for transfer to take place. The recommendations from the 'in practice' section of relevant chapters should be used as a guide. For

**Table 8.1    A template for a diagnostic interview**

| Learning transfer factor | Questions to consider |
|---|---|
| Motivation to learn | Why were you interested in this programme?<br>What were your expectations from it? |
| Training content and design | Was the content relevant to your own job and your training needs?<br>Were there aspects of the programme you found particularly helpful or unhelpful?<br>Did the way in which the programme was delivered make it easier or harder for you to apply what you learned?<br>How does the programme compare with best practice? |
| Motivation to transfer | How keen or otherwise were you to apply what you learned on your return to work?<br>Did you think that applying the new skills would benefit you? |
| Personal ability to transfer | How easy or difficult was it to find time and space to put your new learning into practice?<br>What helped or hindered you in this respect? |
| Manager support and coaching | How helpful or otherwise was your boss with regard to putting what you learned into practice?<br>What did they do or not do? |
| Peer support | How supportive were your peers, either while you were on the programme or when you came back? |
| Organizational climate for transfer | How open or otherwise is your work environment to change?<br>How difficult or otherwise is it to get new things done? |
| Learning outcomes | Did you learn anything you didn't expect to, such as about yourself or your role? |

ease of reference, they are summarized in Table 8.2. More detail is of course available in the relevant chapters.

Some of the actions will no doubt be easier to implement than others. It's also quite possible that a number of practices designed to facilitate learning transfer are already in place. What should be emphasized here is the importance of the managers of training participants in facilitating improvement. They play a very important role both before and after attendance at any learning event. Before the event, their assessment of participants' learning needs, how they might be met and how the resultant learning can be used are critical in generating the motivation to learn. After the event, their role as a coach, as one who can support and challenge new ideas, who can give clear and honest feedback and who can develop their confidence to take on new challenges will significantly help create the necessary time, mental space and opportunity for individuals

## Table 8.2    Improving learning transfer

| Factors to be considered | Actions to be taken |
|---|---|
| Participant motivation to learn<br>• Expectancies regarding usefulness of the training<br>• Job involvement and organizational commitment<br>• Locus of control<br>• Goal orientation<br>• Self-efficacy | Managers can<br>• Work on expectancies<br>• Work on locus of control<br>• Work on goals<br>• Work on commitment<br>• Work on confidence |
| Content and design of the intervention<br>• Training needs analysis<br>• Objectives and outcomes<br>• The balance of theory and practice<br>• Identical elements<br>• Overlearning<br>• Variety of methods<br>• Distributed vs massed learning<br>• Using analogies<br>• Facilitating learning<br>• Action learning<br>• Developing adaptive expertise | Assess the training need<br>Set clear objectives for the training<br>Balance the content in terms of theoretical and practical knowledge<br>Provide relevant reference material<br>Set pre-programme work<br>Deliver the programme in modular form<br>Make the training as relevant to the work situation as possible<br>Vary the training methods and media<br>Provide 'ideas and applications' notebooks<br>Provide opportunities to practise<br>Have participants create an action plan<br>Consider including an action learning component<br>Include some inter-module application work |
| Post-programme activities<br>• Goal setting<br>• Self-management<br>• Relapse prevention<br>• Action planning<br>• Coaching | Promote goal setting (and give sufficient time to it on the programme)<br>Have participants construct an action plan<br>Conduct a self-management session at the end of the programme<br>Encourage participants to meet with their manager<br>Hold refresher/problem-solving sessions<br>Encourage participants to maintain contact with each other<br>Encourage participants to monitor their own behaviour following the programme<br>Review content and learned skills<br>Suggest participants develop a mentoring relationship<br>Consider getting an executive coach<br>Be clear about the purpose of the coaching<br>Decide whether coaching will be stand alone or with a development programme<br>Build coaching into the process from the start<br>Use many sources of information |

**Table 8.2** *Concluded*

| Factors to be considered | Actions to be taken |
|---|---|
| Peer, manager and organizational support<br>• General enthusiasm for change<br>• Listening, questioning, and discussing<br>• Positive and critical feedback<br>• Willingness to 'plug the gaps'<br>• Support from co-participants<br>• Empowerment<br>• Delegation<br>• Using listening and empathy<br>• Creating and maintaining a supportive climate<br>• Communicating effectively<br>• Exerting a wider influence with others<br>• Feedback and coaching<br>• Resources and workloads<br>• Urgency and deadlines<br>• Autonomy and creativity | Use 'buddy' systems<br>Get a 'critical mass' on the same programme<br>Involve managers in the learning process before training<br>Involve managers in the learning process after training<br>Develop managers as coaches<br>Establish pre- and post-training discussions as part of participants' joining instructions<br>Consider refunds of fees/expenses and/or awards<br>Set up post-training presentations to peers and knowledge sharing sessions<br>Hold 'alumni' sessions<br>Establish communities of practice |
| Motivation to transfer<br>• Readiness to learn<br>• Clearly identified needs<br>• Development of greater assertiveness and confidence<br>• Use of a network of co-attendees<br>• Supportive work environment<br>• Learning seen as developmental<br>Personal capacity for transfer<br>• Motivation to transfer<br>• Ability and opportunity to reflect<br>• Using peers and others<br>• Goal setting<br>• Having autonomy<br>• Being assertive | Encourage and allow time for reflection<br>Use peers for support<br>Include coaching as part of the learning process<br>Develop assertiveness<br>Use a learning log<br>Construct a personal development plan |
| Resistance to change<br>• Stakeholders<br>• Organizational culture<br>• Power and politics<br>• Local resistance | Encourage buy-in at appropriate levels<br>Make a business case for the intervention<br>Use adult learning principles<br>Treat the organization's learning disabilities |
| Learning outcomes<br>• Alpha, beta and gamma change | Be aware of different learning outcomes |

to make transfer happen. Overall, their contribution to maintaining a work environment that is conducive to learning is an extremely valuable one.

For this reason, implementation of any plans to improve learning transfer should take the value of this role into account. If managers don't engage in learning transfer-enhancing practices, then the effectiveness of transfer efforts will be greatly diminished. Therefore, on top of other recommendations arising from the diagnosis should be one which seeks to maintain or improve the capabilities of the manager as a coach.

## The Evaluation Phase

Finally, following implementation of changes made as a result of the investigation, an evaluation of those efforts should be carried out after a reasonable length of time has elapsed. Ideally, such a follow-up evaluation will be able to determine if changes made to the learning transfer system have resulted in greater learning transfer from appropriate learning interventions. However, even if learning transfer itself has not been measured (or if the measures aren't considered sufficiently reliable), a repeat of the diagnostic stage will still uncover what has changed in the system. Evaluation was discussed in Chapter 7, and a number of both qualitative and quantitative techniques presented, which can be used either to measure learning transfer or the conditions underlying it.

## In Practice

Below are presented three cases, carried out in different ways for organizations in very different settings. They are intended to illustrate some of the approaches that are available to investigate conditions relating to learning transfer as the starting point for any improvement project. The first investigation used the LTE (described earlier) and was conducted around a middle management development programme for a financial services organization. The second examined the conditions likely to affect a 'manager as coach' programme for a public service agency. It was conducted following a set of pilot workshops, and before the rollout of the workshops to the broader organization. In neither of these cases was learning transfer actually measured. The third report was an attempt to provide evidence for the accuracy of the learning transfer model and highlight some of the more critical factors.

## Case 1: Management Development in Financial Services

The following notes describe the outcome of an analysis of the responses to the Learning Transfer Evaluation questionnaire, administered to 46 participants on the Assistant Manager Development Programme (Eastern Region), the first module of which was delivered recently. Their purpose is to highlight areas of strength and concern around transfer of learning from the programme back to the workplace. It is important to remember that as this is a small sample, some of the figures, particularly those in the middle ranges, need to be treated with caution. Nevertheless, some of the messages are very clear.

From the average score (1–5) for each of the eight scales on the instrument for each participant, it would appear that the programme they attended has been appropriate for their needs, and that in general, there are no major barriers to application of their learning from the programme back at work. However, a closer look at the factor scores will give a more specific picture.

## PROGRAMME CONTENT AND DESIGN

The *programme content and design* (4.09) seems to have met with almost universal approval. In particular, it appears the relevance and practicality of the content was supported by the expertise and credibility of the facilitator(s). In addition, the programme design seems to have given them the opportunity to network with other participants and learn from them. All of these factors are important for transfer.

## MOTIVATION TO LEARN AND LEARNING

Participants' *motivation to learn* (3.62) score is also reasonable. Participants were generally prepared for attendance at the programme and wanted to learn from it (although interestingly, scores relating to the question 'I was free to choose whether or not to attend this programme' ranged from 1 to 5). The score for *learning* (3.80), though respectable, was not as high as that for *programme content and design*. However, this should not be surprising, particularly as development programmes may reflect a broad range of learning needs for the group as a whole, not all of which are of the same degree of relevance to different individuals. This hypothesis is supported by the fact that the average score for *motivation to learn* and for *learning* are very similar. Of interest for this type of programme is that one of the most significant aspects of *learning* reported was that participants gained new insights into themselves and their roles.

## MOTIVATION AND ABILITY TO TRANSFER

Two of the most important factors in terms of application of learning back at work are *motivation to transfer* (3.89) and *personal ability to transfer* (3.65). What prevented the *motivation to transfer* score from being higher overall was a general perception amongst participants that if they didn't use learning from the programme back at work it would not be noticed. Otherwise it was quite high. More importantly, the score for *personal ability to transfer* is reasonably high. A number of things are likely to have accounted for this – the creation of specific action plans, 'being able to find the time to reflect on learning', and where available, support and coaching from their managers (which is discussed below). All of these are critical facilitators of learning transfer.

## THE EFFECT OF WORK ENVIRONMENT FACTORS

Motivation and ability to transfer are in turn affected by a range of other factors – *manager support and coaching* (3.74), *peer support* (3.29), and *organizational climate for transfer* (3.64). The scores for the factors just listed are reasonable, and suggest that while there are no major barriers to transfer, neither is the support from these areas particularly strong. Two points are worth making. Firstly, the scores for *manager support and coaching* represent an uneven distribution of skill in this area amongst managers – some are clearly much better coaches than others. The second point is that in terms of organization support, the score overall for 'I get enough time to do my job' was quite low. However, many participants felt that they could find time to reflect on their learning. Research has demonstrated that those with high *personal ability to transfer* will take these opportunities to reflect wherever they can find them (inside or outside of work), whereas those with lower *personal ability to transfer* may need a greater level of workplace support in this area. Peers do not appear to exert a major influence either way in terms of resistance or support for this group. This may reflect a focus on individual responsibilities within their workplaces, but in any event does not seem to be a major cause for concern.

## SUMMARY

In summary, therefore (once again, bearing in mind the small sample), the conditions for learning transfer from this programme look reasonable. Notwithstanding the comments above, generally speaking, participants have been prepared to attend, learn and apply that learning from what appears to be an appropriate and well-structured programme. Conditions in their work environments are at worst neutral, and in some areas quite supportive of transfer. Under these circumstances, facilitating learning transfer even further would focus on:

- Reinforcing for the managers of participants their support and coaching role before, during and after the programme.

- Ensuring that participants are encouraged to reflect on their learning and how it can be applied (particularly back at work amongst their peers). Their manager can help greatly with this process.

- Continuing to use best practice training techniques that facilitate transfer, such as practical, action-focused learning, the development of adaptive expertise and action planning to turn that learning into changed behaviour.

- Using the issues identified through the questionnaire to help participants reflect on, anticipate and develop strategies to overcome barriers to application and learning transfer.

## Case 2: The Manager as Coach in a Public Agency

Early in 2007, the training and development unit of the agency initiated a series of one-day (with a half-day follow-up) workshops on the subject of coaching, entitled *The Manager as Coach*. There were two main reasons for this initiative. Firstly, a previous management development programme delivered within the agency had identified the importance of coaching as an integral part of the role of the manager. Secondly, a new, upcoming performance management system, shortly to be introduced, was seen as a process in which the practice of coaching of staff by their managers would be an important component. An external training company was engaged to provide a series of workshops. The focus was on positioning coaching firmly within the manager's role and the provision of appropriate skills to enable them to be effective coaches.

The first series of workshops was delivered over a period of 3 months. At that point the training and development unit felt it appropriate to undertake an evaluation of the effectiveness of the workshops to-date. This was partly from a general desire to engage more in evaluation of their training activities, and partly from a more specific need to review the effectiveness of the workshops. It was planned to continue delivery of the workshops to the remainder of managers at that particular grade later that year, and possibly extend it to managers in other grades later. Different methods of evaluation were considered before deciding on a series of semi-structured interviews with a sample of participants, using the model described in this book as a basis. It was felt that this process would enable a more in-depth exploration of relevant factors and thus provide a firmer basis for recommendations. Interviews were conducted with the training provider, the client and a total of 18 participants, chosen at random from amongst those who attended one of the six workshops. The interviews lasted 45–60 minutes on average.

Eight factors central to the effective application of learning from training were investigated, and participants' experience of the effects of these factors was discussed. The investigation also took account of participants' reactions to the workshops and their description of learning and transfer outcomes. Recommendations for improving the effectiveness of the coaching workshop in terms of its impact on participants' application of learning back on-the-job were proposed.

## PARTICIPANT REACTIONS – HOW DID PARTICIPANTS RATE THE WORKSHOPS?

Average ratings for 13 aspects of the workshop for all participants on the first six workshops varied across the sample. Although positive reactions from attendees are no guarantee that learning or transfer will take place, they nevertheless indicated an overall level of satisfaction with the workshop on the day. Highest ratings seemed to reflect the structure and delivery of the workshops and the knowledge and skills of the facilitators. The most important low rating concerned whether the workshops did or didn't meet training objectives. These are discussed more fully later.

## LEARNING AND BEHAVIOUR CHANGE – IS LEARNING FROM TRAINING APPLIED BACK ON-THE-JOB?

Participants interviewed were asked to rate (very roughly and unscientifically) where they thought they might be on a scale of 1–7 in terms of their demonstration of coaching behaviours both before and after the workshop. For the 18 participants, the average difference was an improvement of 0.75. However, nine participants reported no change in their behaviour. One of two reasons was put forward to explain this. Either they felt they were demonstrating the skill adequately before the workshop, or they did not see the need to engage in coaching behaviour. Some other learning outcomes were also mentioned, each by approximately 4–5 participants. They said the workshop had provided a context into which they could place coaching. It also made them more conscious about their management style, and in some of those cases it reinforced their current behaviour as a coach. Additional specific behavioural outcomes were reported. Three participants reported that they now engaged their staff more in seeking solutions to work problems. Three others stated that their working relationship with some of their staff had now taken on a more developmental focus. Examples of the above cited were listening more, delegating more and giving more positive feedback.

Participants' experiences, based on the effects of the eight transfer factors in the framework are now presented.

## MOTIVATION TO LEARN – IS THE WORKSHOP SEEN AS AN OPPORTUNITY TO LEARN AND DEVELOP?

Reactions of participants to being on this workshop varied widely. Ten participants reported that before the workshop they didn't know what to expect from it. Seven of the remainder stated that they attended with an open mind, thinking that it might be useful in some way for them. However, a common reaction throughout, reported specifically in four instances, was 'oh, *another* course'. There was also a feeling expressed by some of the above that '*I'm doing this already*' (and therefore don't need this workshop). An important consideration for this workshop was that all participants interviewed felt they did not have any choice as to whether they attended the workshop or not. Most stated that they were just 'told' to attend, and didn't question it, understanding it was something for all staff at their grade. Only one participant reported that they understood it to be related to the introduction of the new performance management system, despite the fact that the training provider had conducted two briefing sessions within the organization to place the workshops in this context. Low attendance at these briefings may have contributed to this outcome.

## IS THE WORKSHOP CONTENT PERCEIVED AS RELEVANT TO THE JOB?

For seven participants, attendance at the workshop was reported as having the effect of reinforcing something they already knew or did in terms of coaching. Four others suggested that it made them think more about coaching, or helped them better understand the context of that practice. On the other hand, some resistance to the term 'coaching' was expressed. Four participants suggested it was just a '*new label for an old practice*', and two others said that at the end of the workshop they still didn't really understand what coaching actually was. Another opinion expressed in four cases was that this workshop was '*not for me*', suggesting that it would be more appropriate for those at a lower grade, with more (in the opinion of the respondents) people management responsibility. Some particular content areas were mentioned several times as being useful, such as listening and questioning; giving clear direction to staff; communication and encouragement; handing back problems when appropriate; and giving feedback. On the other hand, two participants said they did not fully understand the coaching model used, and two others didn't see its relevance in this situation. Related to this, some people felt that there was too much theory for a workshop of this (short) duration.

## DOES THE DESIGN SHOW IN A PRACTICAL WAY HOW THE TRAINING CAN BE BEST USED?

Quite a variety of opinions were expressed concerning the way in which the workshop was delivered. On the positive side, the role-plays in particular, but also the group work/exercises and the use of participants' own cases to discuss or practise on were highlighted in nine cases. In addition, two participants cited the follow-up workshop as useful in helping them focus on the application of learning. On the negative side, two participants reported feeling uncomfortable during the role-plays, and stated that they felt they didn't reflect *'real life'*. One exercise in particular was mentioned by six participants as being of limited relevance. Those participants felt the message it was meant to convey was lost along the way.

## MOTIVATION TO TRANSFER – DOES THE PARTICIPANT HAVE A DESIRE TO APPLY THE LEARNING?

Twelve participants reported what could be regarded as a high or medium level of motivation to transfer their learning from the workshop back to their job, and six reported low or none.

## PERSONAL CAPACITY FOR TRANSFER – CAN THE PARTICIPANT MAKE THE 'MENTAL SPACE' TO APPLY THE LEARNING?

Four participants felt that they would be willing to apply learning from this workshop (and any others) if they could clearly see a practical application for it. Another condition that would make it easier to do this would be the opportunity to reflect on what was learned. Participants who found that opportunity (sometimes at work, sometimes outside work) were generally those who had more autonomy in their work. Those who found transfer more difficult reported operational priorities and lack of time as inhibitors.

## ORGANIZATIONAL SUPPORT FOR TRANSFER – DO ORGANIZATIONAL FACTORS ENABLE OR INHIBIT THE USE OF NEW LEARNING?

Overall, a strong feeling was expressed (10 participants) that the agency is supportive of education and development, primarily demonstrated through provision of funding for external courses. However, this did not seem to extend to other forms of support within the workplace, such as job-related follow up to courses or any processes for facilitating the transfer of learning. Mentioned on five occasions was the fact that shortages of staff resources can make it difficult to give the time to transfer. Importantly, as regards internal training, three participants felt there was a lack of connection between the courses provided and the type of training they felt was needed.

## MANAGER SUPPORT AND COACHING – IS THERE HELP OR HINDRANCE FROM THE BOSS IN APPLYING NEW LEARNING?

The strong overall impression created (reported specifically in five cases) was that managers of participants did not see any role for themselves in supporting the application of learning. Although two participants had a post-course meeting with their boss, the remainder of the responses indicated a lack of interest generally, sometimes even a lack of awareness that the participant had actually been on a training course, and consequently no discussion of how the learning acquired might be applied back at work. This contrasted with three interviews in which participants stated that they generally try to support their own staff in transferring learning.

## PEER SUPPORT – IS THERE HELP OR HINDRANCE FROM PEERS IN APPLYING NEW LEARNING?

There was not a lot of peer influence reported by any participant. Responses of workplace peers were described as indifferent, often where the peer was not aware that the participant had attended a training workshop at all. However, some support was forthcoming from co-attendees at the workshop, where two participants in particular reported that they now had a contact in another part of the agency to whom they might refer in the future.

## ORGANIZATIONAL CLIMATE FOR TRANSFER – IS THERE RELUCTANCE IN THE WORK ENVIRONMENT TO TRY NEW WAYS OF DOING THINGS?

In general, work environments were seen as broadly supportive of change. Nine participants in particular suggested that their workplaces were positive towards change. However, none of the participants' work environments were described as dynamic in terms of initiating change, tending to be more reactive.

## SOME OBSERVATIONS

The above results present the main comments made by those chosen for the sample. All the comments reported so far were made by more than one person. However, taking these and other individual comments into consideration, a number of observations can be made.

Firstly, there is the issue of mandatory attendance at the workshop. As stated earlier, all participants interviewed understood that the workshop was a training requirement for people at their grade. While this was no doubt the case for a significant proportion of that group, there were also participants interviewed who had either already received significant training in this area, or (as in the case of at least two participants) didn't actually have any staff reporting to them. As a result, within each workshop there was a range of differing training needs, with consequent difficulties in terms of positioning the workshop. Secondly, and related to the first issue, is that the rationale for the workshop and its content did not have the opportunity to be discussed (apart perhaps from the poorly-attended briefings) until participants were actually in attendance. Being in a position to do this in the workplace beforehand would have improved participants' motivation to learn, and thus their motivation to transfer that learning. This issue is particularly important in the light of the number of people who felt the workshop was *'not for me'* or *'more suitable for others'*, or that coaching was not a part of their job. Whether they are right or wrong, appropriate discussion of why they should attend the workshop would enable highlighting of these questions. A distinct impression (related to the two issues above) formed during the interviews was that within the agency, coaching is about managing poor performers only, and seen more as disciplinary in nature. This view is at odds with the one presented at the start of the workshop where, according to the workshop facilitators (and backed up by output on flipcharts), participants identified a broader range of aspects to coaching. What is likely in that instance is that participants were identifying what it *should* look like in theory, rather than identifying what it *does* look like in their experience.

Whether it represents reality or not, there would appear to be a distinct perception of a lack of connection within the agency between the training that is delivered and the real training needs that exist. Evidence for this comes from the high number of participants for whom the 'invitation' to attend the workshop was the first suggestion to them of a need for competence in coaching. Other factors investigated during the interview process also lend support to this assertion. For instance, most participants reported a level of indifference or even ignorance amongst their managers concerning their participation on the workshop (the same was true for training in general). Evidence from the interviews suggests that few if any managers within the agency see facilitating the transfer of learning of their staff as part of their role. Nor does the agency itself to any great extent, given that its support for learning and development consists of providing funding, rather than installing any structures to support learning back at work. Finally, the lack of any incentives to apply learning, or indeed sanctions for not applying it, suggest that transfer of learning is largely left to chance.

## RECOMMENDATIONS

Based on the above research and observations, as well as what constitutes best practice in training and development, a number of recommendations are now put forward. However, rather than provide a long list of initiatives that may be unrealistic to implement in the present circumstances, the focus instead is on changes to the current system that are more straightforward, yet which should have a real impact on the effectiveness of the workshops. These recommendations are discussed in terms of what should be done before, during and after the workshop.

*Before the workshop* Perhaps at the core of the difficulties described above is the way in which internal training is organized. At the moment, it seems that training in general is quite grade-related, rather than provided in response to needs identified in any other way. It is not known from the interviews in what way training needs are identified internally. Best practice, however, would suggest that this be a transparent process, involving staff (for example in focus groups) at as many levels as is practicable. This has the multiple effect of identifying needs that reflect the reality of employees' jobs, clearer identification of target populations and helping to promote your training activity at the same time.

More specifically, to avoid the situation whereby future participants know little or nothing about the training workshop they are about to attend, it is recommended that intending participants are sent an 'invitation' letter to join the workshop, outlining the purpose and nature of the workshop, and asking them to have a meeting with their boss prior to attending. The purpose of this meeting is to bring the boss 'into the loop' and to identify if and how the proposed training is likely to be of benefit. If it can be shown that the individual is not likely to benefit from the training, then the option for them not to attend should exist. This pre-workshop meeting also ensures that the boss is aware that the training is taking place, and encourages them to see supporting it as part of their role. If it is not already the case, the crucial role of the boss in the development of individuals and consequently improved performance should be emphasized in their own training.

*During the workshop*   In order to ensure the best chance of the learning from the workshop surviving the transition to the workplace, the practical design of the workshop should be maintained. Given the short duration of the workshop, the concentration should be on practical application (such as in role-plays, using where possible situations experienced in real life by participants) even if at the expense of some of the 'theory'. If necessary, more time should be spent at the outset of the workshop to position it within the culture of the agency, particularly its role within performance management, which may be perceived as new. It would add weight if this introduction was provided by a member of senior management. At the end of the workshop, it is important to maintain the practical action plan – the conducting of a coaching session along specific guidelines. As well as supporting transfer and providing a focus for the follow-up workshop (which incidentally should be advertised as an integral part of the workshop if that is not already the case), it is an opportunity for trainees to enlist the support of their manager.

*After the workshop*   The importance of a post-workshop meeting with the participant's boss has already been emphasized. This meeting would allow discussion of learning and application of that learning back at work. One additional option (suggested by more than one participant) would be to ask the trainee to make a short presentation to other staff members concerning the training and its use. To improve the chances of learning transfer, an important post-training activity is to have follow-up sessions. These sessions, which may be as short as 2 hours, and which typically take place a number of months after an initial training intervention, can be used to focus on application of learning outcomes and take into account specific conditions and needs in particular workplaces. Participants' action plans, successes and difficulties in implementing them can be the starting point for these sessions. Therefore as a component of the current coaching programme they should be retained. Further follow-up if necessary should be at local level.

## CONCLUSION

Delivering effective training and development is dependent upon a number of different factors. While training content and design are very important, it has been seen that the successful application of learning back at work also requires other conditions to exist, particularly the creation of motivation to and capacity for transfer, a role in which the participant's manager can play a major part. Some of these conditions are easier to change than others. Nevertheless, it is hoped that the practical and feasible changes recommended above will make a start on this process and ultimately lead to a better return for the efforts of all those engaged in training and development activity.

# Case 3: Factors Underlying High and Low Transfer

## INTRODUCTION

As a means of demonstrating whether the set of relationships proposed in the learning transfer model might reflect participants' reality, some individual cases were looked at as part of a broader study of learning transfer from a leadership development programme based around a set of relevant competencies. Notwithstanding the fact that it is very difficult to attribute transfer clearly to factors discussed in the study, given its complex nature, the following was undertaken. Using a variation on the Success Case Method (Brinkerhoff 2006), the highest and lowest overall scores on the LTE were determined by summing the responses to all questions. Next, the highest and lowest overall gains on the competency profile instrument (a measure of learning transfer) were determined in the same way. This was to see if particular patterns might emerge (for example, to see if individuals might be at the higher or lower end of either scale simultaneously).

Six participants were identified in this way. On one hand, three participants were among the highest scorers on the LTE, indicating a set of factors positive towards the transfer of learning. At the same time, scores for these individuals indicated a higher degree of learning transfer. Similarly, three others were identified where conditions for transfer were among the lowest reported, and who reported a lower degree of transfer. Their six 'stories' (as described in the interviews) were mapped on to the model, to see if there were relevant relationships or if other insights might be gained. These cases will now be discussed.

## HIGH TRANSFER CASES

There are a number of similarities among the cases where the degree of transfer was high and the conditions were favourable for transfer. To begin with, as with all other participants, they considered the content relevance and the quality of programme delivery to be very high. In addition, their level of motivation to learn was no different to the majority of others. However, unlike many other participants, each of the three placed great emphasis on their own ability to transfer learning should they want to, and reported a high level of self-efficacy. Each felt that despite what was going on around them (either personally or professionally), they accepted that achieving change in their behaviour at work would be largely 'up to themselves'. In fact two of the three cases reported successful handling of recent significant personal trauma, which they suggested may have helped in their perception of their ability to meet a challenge such as transferring learning. For instance: 'I'm saying to people, if you want to do anything you can't depend on the organization to help you in your training and development, you have to show that you are willing to go and do it yourself.' There was evidence that this high level of self-efficacy demonstrated, together with positive perceptions of the programme design and its relevance, combined to create a desire to make use of the learning in the 'real world', that is, motivation to transfer. The next step for them was to create the space in their working life for this to happen. In the three cases, their scores on personal ability to transfer were among the highest overall. Thus for these three, their levels of performance self-efficacy, motivation to transfer and personal ability to transfer were amongst the highest of all participants.

On the other hand, the pattern of work environment influences for these cases is not significantly different from others. For instance, in two of the three cases, their immediate boss was considered distinctly unsupportive. The boss of the third was neither supportive nor unsupportive. As one said: 'It was more a case of they would be happy to let a participant or a person who had been on a programme apply new learning as long as it did not get in the way of whatever the boss was doing.' In addition, the amount of support provided by peers varied widely amongst the three, as did the amount of feedback and coaching they got from various sources. This would seem to lend support for the greater importance of individual factors in enabling transfer.

## LOW TRANSFER CASES

When comparisons are made between the group just discussed and the three participants whose scores were among the lowest on the LTE, and who reported the least amount of transfer (no transfer), some interesting observations can be made. Notwithstanding the difficulties in measuring transfer described above, for those for whom the degree of transfer was lowest, perceptions concerning transfer design and validity of the content were both high in the case of one and both low in the case of another. As with other participants, their level of self-efficacy also varied. In fact one of the three had one of the highest scores on that dimension. However, all three individuals appeared in the bottom four in terms of both their level of motivation to transfer and their level of personal ability to transfer. This again points to a strong link between motivation and personal ability to transfer.

Part of this effect may be due to their perception of content validity – two of the three were among the lowest scoring in this respect. However, despite what was going on around them, the lower scoring individuals reported finding it more difficult to 'make the space' to transfer. They reported more hindrances to their motivation to transfer learning, such as: 'One of the things, obviously… if we had backup support that would be one thing that would help make changes and new things we learn easier.' However, the low scores concerning their perceptions of content validity may have more to do with their understanding of their roles. Two of the three in particular felt strongly that the 'people-related' aspects of their job were a distraction from the more 'task-related' elements, and did not see the former as an integral part of the job. 'I would find that I would be dealing with so many of their personal problems and everything else. I should be involved in the budgeting, that sort of thing. I should have time to follow up on all these things. I don't.' This perception is all the more important as they in fact reported more supportive bosses than those with the highest transfer scores, and equivalent amounts of organizational support also. This can be linked to motivation and personal capacity for transfer in that perhaps they weren't motivated to become a 'people manager' and thus didn't feel the need to make the space for the people-related elements, considering them as they did outside their normal range of responsibilities.

## Summary

The evidence presented from a wealth of studies and experience over the decades certainly indicates that some degree of learning transfer takes place following most learning and development interventions. However, the nature of this transfer will be different for different individuals. For some, change will be a straightforward change in some aspect of their knowledge or skill. For others, the intervention may change completely how they think about a subject.

We have also seen that a large number of factors can affect the transfer of learning, exerting varying degrees of effects. In terms of specific factors, the evidence points to the central role of *motivation to transfer* in the overall process, given that it is significantly related to more factors than any other. On some occasions, factors work with each other in exerting their effect on *motivation to transfer*, while on other occasions they act independently. For instance, *programme content and design* works to provide confidence for participants to apply what they learn on their return to work. Similarly, clarity and constructive *manager support and coaching* from supportive managers and peers back at work helps these individuals see how learning might be applied, and the potential benefits. *Motivation to transfer* is also a major component of the total effect on *personal ability to transfer*. *Motivation to transfer* represents the 'desire' to transfer, whilst *personal ability to transfer* represents the 'ability' to transfer. The close relationship between these factors, the direction of that relationship, and the relative strength of correlations with learning transfer suggest that *motivation to transfer* (and to a lesser extent *personal ability to transfer*) is activated by a number of factors in the work environment. This in turn influences the individual's *personal ability to transfer*, enabling transfer to take place. Both factors (but particularly the latter) are affected by the level of *manager support and coaching* available and the *organizational climate for transfer*, which has the effect of helping to 'make the space' to transfer learning.

The fact that *personal ability to transfer* appears to exert the strongest effect on learning transfer may highlight an underestimated role for some of the post-training transfer strategies discussed. Strategies such as goal setting, self-management and in particular coaching all involve working on some aspect of the trainee's personal ability to transfer learning. They achieve this through encouraging reflection on learning, anticipating difficulties with regard to its application and formulating ways of dealing with these difficulties. There is also clear evidence of interaction between various factors in the model. Within the work environment the factors *peer support*, *manager support* and *feedback and coaching* contain similar elements, and the evidence supports their role in increasing confidence and motivation. In particular, manager behaviour (including reinforcing training and giving performance feedback) has a strong influence on the level of resistance or openness to change in a work environment. Finally, the fact that so many factors in the model correlate significantly with *motivation to transfer* may suggest a common mechanism at work, most likely through their effect on self-efficacy.

## A Final Word

It is clear from the literature and from learning and development practice that a range of factors affects the transfer of learning from the classroom to the workplace. Through proper diagnosis and focused interventions these factors can be manipulated in order to increase the amount of transfer. By increasing the amount of transfer, organizations can improve the rate of return on resources spent on training and development from what is still a very low base (recall that most estimates have typically been in the 10 per cent to 20 per cent range). To achieve this, they need to consider transfer in a structured way, working to increase the effect of the facilitating factors and reduce the effect of the inhibiting factors. Only in this way will investment in the capabilities necessary to deliver competitive advantage be realized.

## References

Brinkerhoff, R.O. (2006). Increasing impact of training investments: An evaluation strategy for building organizational learning capability. *Industrial and Commercial Training,* 38(6), 302–07.

# APPENDIX A:
# Understanding Learning Transfer from a Management Development Programme

## Introduction

The purpose of this chapter is to describe in detail the process of learning transfer from a study conducted around one particular management development programme. A summary of discussions with a sample of participants on the programme is provided, illustrating their perceptions concerning how the process of learning transfer worked for them, and reinforcing the effects of learning transfer factors discussed in previous chapters.

## Research Setting

The results reported are part of a study into understanding the process of learning transfer as experienced by participants on a management development programme within a health service setting. A total of 112 managers took part in one of four separate programmes, all delivered by the same provider. The programmes were aimed at middle managers, and were presented in modular form involving 12 days over a period of 6 months. Broadly speaking, the objectives to be achieved for the programme were:

- The development of an understanding of current trends, innovations and managerial best practice in nursing and health service management.

- Clarification of participants' role within the management team.

- Strategic and service planning, policy formulation, quality assurance and clinical effectiveness.

- Resource management expertise, including budgeting skills, workforce management, and identification of staff education and development requirements.

- Personal development planning to guide their current and ongoing development.

- The development of clinical leadership skills.

- Staff management skills, including the motivation, coaching and empowerment of staff; the handling of grievance and discipline; staff development and facilitation of personal career planning; negotiating and influencing.

In terms of programme design, a number of elements to enhance learning and transfer were incorporated (based on recommendations from a review of the pilot programme), including a focus on small group work, in particular the use of action learning sets; the completion and monitoring of reflective journals; one-to-one coaching, in particular around a personal development plan (PDP); a work-based project; significant time for action planning; and feedback on a competency profile designed specially for this group of managers.

## Collecting the Data

Data for this part of the study were collected by means of semi-structured interviews. The main question to be answered was how the process operated – whether participants felt that transfer had or had not taken place, and in particular, what the action of the various factors looked like in practice. It was also important to find out under what conditions learning transfer took place; whether some factors were more important than others; what their effects were; and how participants dealt with them. To gather this information, it was decided that a semi-structured format that included an interview guide to provide some structure would be best. This helped to systematize the collection of data across different sites and facilitated comparisons during the analysis.

It also facilitated the important aim of '... gaining full access to the knowledge and meanings of the respondents' (Seale 1999), who suggests recording observations as concretely as possible, and including verbatim accounts rather than researchers' general reconstructions. Furthermore he recommends tape-recording interviews, carefully transcribing them and presenting long extracts of data in the research report. So, in order to maintain reliability and gain access to what respondents thought and understood, the interviews were tape-recorded and subsequently transcribed.

The interview content and process were developed with the primary aims of: (a) ensuring coverage of the main factors understood from the literature to influence learning transfer; and (b) allowing room for raising and discussing any other issues thought relevant by participants to the process of transfer. In addition to these, the time spent with the interviewee was also to be used as an opportunity to collect their perceptions of the extent of learning transfer that had taken place (by means of the summary section of a specially designed competency profile) and other background data, such as their areas of accountability, job responsibilities and number of reports. It was proposed that in the interview, gathering of background data would be done first in order to put interviewees at ease and 'get them talking'. Open questions around participants' experience of the development programme, the learning that took place for them and their experience of trying to put that learning into practice back at work were prepared, to be asked next. Follow-up questions, seeking more detail and/or specific examples of issues raised, were also planned. At all times, the range of factors known to affect transfer was in the mind of the researcher so that if mentioned by the interviewee, they could be followed up on. Finally, questions around what the participants themselves might do as a manager to encourage learning transfer in their own areas of responsibility, as well as an invitation to discuss any issues thought relevant and not already discussed were also prepared. An interview template provided this structure around which to work in the interviews.

In the end, a total of 27 participants were interviewed for the study. Participants on the programme came from organizations in all regions of the country. These organizations included large and small hospitals, care of the elderly facilities, schools for children with learning difficulties and public health offices. Length of service in the current job varied from a few weeks to 2 years, although all participants had several years of technical experience behind them. The number of staff these people were ultimately responsible for was rarely less than 20, and typically up to 70. There was also a wide spectrum of accountabilities. The group contained a number of operating theatre managers, accident and emergency unit managers, outpatient clinic managers, ward managers and managers of other acute and long-term care services.

The data from the interviews were coded along the dimensions of the factors described in the model in Chapter 1. Additional data were sought during the interview concerning participants' opinions of the type and amount of transfer of learning to the workplace that had taken place. They were asked questions around what (if anything) they were now doing differently at work as a result of having attended the programme. They were also asked about the design of the development programme and the extent of support they received from their peers, their own managers and the organization as a whole. They were encouraged to discuss anything else they thought might be of relevance to the issue of learning transfer. This provided valuable insights into the process of transfer as experienced by each of these individuals.

The research interviews took place over a period of 4 weeks, some months after completion of the programme. By that time, participants would have had plenty of opportunity to put into practice their learning from the programme, or would have given up trying to do so. All interviews were conducted by the same researcher. Participants were very happy to discuss their experience of the programme and its effect on their work despite their busy schedules. The interviews themselves were very informal, and interviewees settled into them without any difficulty. Interviews lasted on average between 60 and 90 minutes, and covered participants' experience of attending the programme, its highlights and deficiencies, the competency framework around which the programme was structured and, in particular, the facilitators and inhibitors encountered in trying to put learning from the programme into practice back at work. Following further reassurance concerning the confidentiality of data collected, each interview was tape recorded to ensure accuracy and to allow the researcher to concentrate on the flow of the interview and the information being given. The interviews took place at the participants' workplace, and in some cases were accompanied by a tour of the participant's area of responsibility. This made it easier to put many of the comments into context. For example, two interviews took place in accident and emergency units, against a background of noise, constant movement and unavoidable interruption, characteristic of these highly operationally-focused environments. By contrast, three others took place in environments such as care of the elderly or palliative care facilities, where the nature and consequent pace of work was altogether different. In a different way, disparities in resources available to some organizational units managed by interviewees were reflected in the offices and other rooms in which the interviews took place. Finally, some sense of the climate of the work unit was also obtained while observing human interactions during waiting time before the interviews. The interviews were transcribed by an associate and the resulting output comprised some 250 pages of text, which was then analyzed using Atlas/Ti.

## Coding the Responses

The interview data were coded in accordance with the factors described in the model in Chapter 1. Quotations were assigned to relevant codes (sometimes more than one). Other codes not covered by the model were also added, relating to factors such as deeper learning, demographic information and comments regarding the competency framework. In the course of the analysis, a number of passes were made through the data and some recoding took place, better reflecting what was meant in the light of other knowledge. Coding the responses in this way enabled the researcher to map the experiences of respondents directly on to the model, while at the same time retaining flexibility with regard to other issues that might arise in the course of the interview. The issues examined in this way, and which together describe the process of transfer as experienced by the participants, are discussed now under each of the code headings.

## Motivation to Learn: The Degree to which Individuals are Prepared to Enter and Participate in the Programme

Different descriptions of motivation to learn (Quinones and Ehrenstein 1996) relate to whether individuals decide to attend a training programme in the first place, or the amount of effort they exert during the training. Based on this assumption, the results seen here therefore concurred with the first part of Colquitt, LePine and Noe's (2000) model outlined in Chapter 1. In that model, factors that affected motivation to learn were pre-training self-efficacy, valence (perceptions regarding the potential usefulness of the training) and job/career variables such as job involvement and organizational commitment. All of these factors may have been at work here. There is further support for this position in that the only other factor with which motivation to learn had a significant correlation for this group was motivation to transfer.

## PRE-TRAINING SELF-EFFICACY

Pre-training self-efficacy in general was high – all participants when asked stated clearly that they had no reservations at all about their ability to complete the programme and learn from it. All of them had received third-level education, significant clinical training, and 12 of them had previously attended more general programmes on different aspects of management. Part of their self-efficacy may also be explained by the fact that a significant number of participants felt that they were being 'singled out' (in a positive way) and 'treated' in some way by being asked to participate in the programme. Having said that, of the 10 participants who made reference to the fact that they had been asked to attend, none of them felt in any way that they were being coerced to do so. In fact, they reported the opposite.

## JOB INVOLVEMENT

The reasons the participants were chosen for the programme may also be related to job involvement and commitment. As reported earlier in the literature review, both Tesluk et al. (1995) and Facteau et al. (1995) found organizational commitment and positive attitudes to jobs to be related to transfer intentions and actual transfer. Nomination to attend the programme was seen, if not actually as a reward, at least as some sort of recognition of job commitment. This programme was a second pilot programme for a new management development initiative. All participants were approached (usually through nomination by their director) to take part in the programme, rather than it being something they applied for in the normal way. It was in their organization's interest to 'get the programme off to a good start' by having people who wanted to gain from the programme participate in it. This perception was helped by the fact that the four participants who discussed this issue reported that their own managers presented the opportunity to attend as a future-oriented opportunity rather than a remedial action.

## PERCEPTIONS OF USEFULNESS

The overall level of valence, that is, the perception of potential usefulness of the programme, too, was high amongst all participants. This should not be surprising, given the circumstances of their involvement in the programme explained above. Studies by both Hicks and Klimowski (1987), and Baldwin, Magjuka and Loher (1991) have suggested that these high 'expectancies' will increase participants' motivation to learn. It is most likely that this perception was a general one, relating to an opportunity to learn something new and useful, rather than a content-specific one, as most participants did not know what to expect in terms of content before the programme began. Five participants expressed the feeling that 'they needed something', without being very specific about what it was. Indications from the interviews support the view that the specific content was not of primary importance to most participants. They knew it was a management development programme, and many of them had expressed a strong need to undertake management development to support them in their new role, which for most of them was still evolving. Given that this programme was focused specifically on management issues for this group of people, it provided an important opportunity in that regard. Seven of those interviewed made particular reference to the fact they had little or no idea of the content of the programme before they began it. However, given who was behind it, and feeling that it would be a good developmental opportunity, they said they approached the programme in a positive frame of mind. Just over half the participants knew what to expect from the programme in terms of content. They were 'ready' in the sense that the programme as described matched felt management development needs, and they hoped it would either show them new ways of managing, or reinforce their current management practice. Apart from specific programme content, the desire to attend to get to know a network of other managers in similar situations was quite strong. Twelve participants interviewed revealed expectations such as the following. 'I suppose what I looked forward to most about the course was meeting people in the same position as myself and maybe from the same [work] area as myself as well as from the broader service, and I suppose to just be given a chance to see what difficulties they have.'

## Programme Content and Design: The Degree to Which Design and Delivery of the Programme Make it Easier to Transfer Learning

Given that the motivation to learn from the programme was so widespread, it is not surprising that many participants' perceptions of the content (first of all) were that it was quite valid. The main contributing factor to the favourable perception of content validity was the fact that a comprehensive pre-programme needs analysis and post-programme evaluation of the first pilot programme, completed earlier the same year, had been conducted. The evaluation of the original pilot programme identified the most relevant content areas and made suggestions for future programmes. Most of these recommendations were adopted for this programme. Studies such as that of Baldwin, Magjuka and

Loher (1991) reinforce the positive effect on transfer of having training content congruent with job requirements.

## VALID CONTENT

Six positive reports were received concerning the practical nature of the programme content. Those participants felt that issues dealt with and exercises used related directly to their own areas of work, and could see how the resultant learning could be applied, citing the use of real-life scenarios as being particularly valuable. The areas most consistently mentioned were those concerned with the management of people, such as conflict handling, communicating, influencing, giving feedback and conducting effective meetings (18 reports). Budgeting (6) and service planning (5) were also regularly mentioned. All of these areas were seen to be particularly relevant to the current job of these managers. In addition to declarative knowledge, specific procedural knowledge and skills in the above areas were also imparted (Clark 1990). For half of the participants, these skills and knowledge were reported as being new. These were people who, despite some practical experience of managing, had not as yet been exposed to other formal management skills training. For the other half, it was seen as an endorsement of what they already knew (either from experience or from previous training) or of the way they managed. The only reported difference between the two groups was that the latter now felt that they had a framework (that is, the declarative knowledge) into which to place their (procedural) knowledge and skills. Having this framework gave them confidence that what they were already doing was in fact good practice. The positive effect on transfer of increased confidence was reported earlier by Smith and Ragan (1993). To quote a case, 'It helped me I would suppose to reinforce what was right and what I thought about how to manage people and how to operate.' Three cases were reported where participants felt that the content was not relevant at the time of attendance at the programme, but in fact later found it to be useful. One example was, 'There was one thing that we did, evidence-based research. I found that very, very, useful. But if I had been told that going on the course, I might not see it as all that relevant to me.' Some of these later 'discoveries' can be related to the nature of the training content. Some of the aims of the programme included providing clarification of the role of the manager in that particular environment, as well as insights into one's own style and personality. As is often the case with development programmes, these may take time to be understood and accepted. So, participants' perceptions of content validity have a part to play in terms of their satisfaction with the programme. In addition, these perceptions have been seen to be important in terms of stimulating motivation to learn (Baldwin, Magjuka and Loher 1991).

## GOOD DESIGN

The actual design of the programme is another important issue, which received universal approval. The most frequently reported reason for this (it was mentioned specifically 19 times in interviews) was the opportunity the programme structure afforded participants to learn from and receive support from others. This was achieved in two ways. Firstly, there was an emphasis placed on using action learning sets and practical problems as a basis for learning. Eleven participants made mention of the usefulness of this technique. Secondly, there was the general interaction (both during course hours and outside them) that is facilitated by being on a residential programme. In general, participants themselves supplied the work-related management problems on which the groups worked. Working in small groups on these problems (Marsick and O'Neil 1999; Jennings 2002) had the benefit of helping provide real solutions that could be tried out and reported back on. While small group working was considered effective, the opportunities for learning and support within the larger group were also extremely important. Almost every participant reported deriving at least some benefit from the opportunity to share experiences with others, with more than 20 participants reporting on the benefits of networking opportunities provided by the way the programme was structured. This seems to have helped different people in different ways. For some, it was a matter of providing practical solutions to their own work-based problems. For others, if this process did not actually provide solutions to problems, it often provided support, either in the individual's understanding of the problem, their view of it, or perhaps an endorsement of their way of dealing with it. This learning often happened within the learning sets themselves. It also happened in the many group discussions that were a part of the programme design. In addition, the residential nature of the programme ensured that participants also had plenty of opportunity to meet informally. Four participants reported using opportunities to discuss work-related issues on such occasions as over coffee, in the bar or walking in the hotel grounds.

Formal or informal discussion about work-related issues often produced advice on a particular problem. Three examples reported concerned problems of budgeting, service planning and dealing with difficult staff. These participants felt they could now deal with their issues back at work with more confidence, and at least knew that they were not the only manager with such issues to contend with. The number of times the word 'confidence' was used in this context (it was used on 35 occasions in all) indicates that helping to raise (or maintain) the person's performance self-efficacy was at work here (Stevens and Gist, 1997; Carlson et al. 2000). In effect, the type of support offered was peer support, with perhaps some feedback and coaching (Peters and O'Connor 1980; Rouiller and Goldstein 1993).

## GOOD FACILITATION

Another transfer design issue was the credibility of the facilitators (mentioned by five participants). Between them they demonstrated significant knowledge of the world in which the managers worked. This worked together with their facilitative style ('facilitation of learning' rather than 'teaching') to make a positive impact. What participants most frequently mentioned (on seven occasions) as helpful was the 'adult learning' approach taken (MacDonald, Gabriel and Cousins 2000). Furthermore, the facilitators drew a lot on participants' current knowledge and experience as a basis for learning. Reports concerning the skills of the facilitators considered it important that they drew a balance between bringing issues to the surface so that they could be discussed openly, and setting ground rules that ensured confidentiality was maintained within the group. The three participants who discussed achieving this balance felt it helped to generate trust in the facilitators' ability, which in turn helped participants' satisfaction with the learning process. As one respondent put it, '...you have to tap into the group if you want it to work. There was a degree of flexibility in the programme and for me I would have to say there was a variety of people with a variety of experience and skills, about 30 people, and I thought that everybody in that room was actually facilitated very well'.

## OTHER DESIGN ISSUES

Yet another transfer design factor, supported in the research (Naylor and Briggs 1983), was the 'distributed' nature of the training. There were several weeks between modules. In addition to using this time to advance their work-related project, participants were often required to 'try out' something they had learned, such as chairing a meeting or giving feedback to a staff member. They were then in a position to report back to their learning set at the next module, and use it for guidance and support. Six participants stated they found this design feature positive. Even if such opportunities didn't occur, participants also had a 'reflective journal' (for noting new ideas, thoughts and applications) to facilitate thinking about learning. An important component of some approaches to action learning (Marsick and O'Neil 1999), the importance of creating this 'reflective time' should not be underestimated. Formalizing the process of reflection helped make it a little easier to do, thus facilitating transfer. This was particularly important to do, as evidence from the interviews points to difficulty in creating this reflective time outside of the programme. This issue will be discussed more fully under 'personal ability to transfer'.

## Motivation to Transfer: The Direction and Persistence of Effort in Applying Back at Work Skills and Knowledge Learned

Based on the level of attention it has received in the literature, motivation to transfer is a very important factor in the transfer of learning. Both Colquitt, LePine and Noe's (2000) meta-analysis and Ford and Weissbein's (1997) review of transfer research point to its central importance in the transfer process. For the 27 participants interviewed following this programme, motivation to transfer was very high overall. Among the participants interviewed, the following themes emerged repeatedly. There were reasons put forward for a lack of motivation to transfer also, which, unsurprisingly, were the opposite of some of the reasons advanced below:

- They were ready to learn. In all, 11 participants reported having been waiting for just such a programme as this to assist them in their role as manager.

- There was a perceived need identified in many workplaces for the skills and knowledge taught on the programme, as well as a desire on the part of some participants to develop a particular management style. This was discussed in 12 cases. Those participants reported the usefulness of the competency framework and of feedback from others in identifying development needs.

- Related to the above was a recognition (reported by four participants) of the need to manage change within their areas of influence, for which a broader picture of their management role and its challenges was seen as necessary.

- Seven individuals said they felt better able for the challenge of transfer, through having developed greater assertiveness and confidence by virtue of their learning and their interactions with others on the programme.

- A number of the issues discussed earlier in terms of transfer design and content, particularly the applicability of programme content, were raised again by five participants. They reported that it encouraged them to look at training issues in the light of their own work situation and problems.

- Those (three) participants who felt that they would have a reasonable length of time to implement changes (for example, through being permanent rather than temporary in their posts) in their own workplaces were more motivated to transfer.

- Six of those who looked on the invitation to be part of the programme as some recognition of their efforts to-date reported they felt more motivated to transfer.

## Personal Ability to Transfer: The Extent to which Individuals have the Time, Energy and Mental Space in their Work Lives to Make Changes Required to Transfer Learning to the Job

Based on responses from participants who discussed it, the most frequently cited issue in this category was that of reflection. Reflection as a facilitating factor in transfer appears in the use of such tools as self-management (Brown and Latham 2000), relapse prevention (Burke 1997) and coaching (Sloan 2001). Being able to reflect on what participants learn on the programme and making changes to their behaviour is seen as an important part of making the training work.

In total, nine participants made reference to both the need for and the difficulty of finding time to reflect on learning. Many work environments, due to the nature of the work carried out (for example, operating theatres, accident and emergency units) were not at all conducive to such a practice. Furthermore, few of these managers had the luxury of being able stand back from the day-to-day work, as they were also 'working' members of their teams. First of all, in order to reflect, six participants reported having to find opportunities to do so outside work, for example at home, while driving or in the garden. Another strategy three participants reported was using their peers at work. For example, peers were asked to cover for an individual while the latter spent time on a future-oriented application of learning, such as a redesign of the appraisal system, or the writing of a service plan. They felt the benefit of this support was further enhanced where the peer had attended a similar programme, or better still, the same programme. Peer support will be discussed more fully later, but in cases where peers also attended the programme, they served as 'buddies' with whom participants could discuss application of learning, give each other feedback, and in general help create the 'space' for transfer. The encouragement of networking, which was an important part of the transfer design could also be playing a part here. Despite this support, time to reflect was still reported as difficult to achieve. In four situations, particularly where work environment factors such as manager support were not strong, participants chose to link up with a mentor, a practice recommended but not enforced in the programme design. What this at least did was formalize some time when the participant could reflect on learning and identify application and problem-solving strategies. It also provided an opportunity for them to get some further feedback, advice or support.

It was reported in the discussion concerning transfer design that only one individual made specific mention of action planning (conducted at the end of the programme) as being useful as a transfer strategy. This was surprising because the practice of goal setting (an important part of any action planning activity) has been shown to facilitate transfer (Magjuka, Baldwin and Loher 1994; Brown and Latham 2000). The person who felt action planning to be useful in helping her transfer learning reported that as well as providing specificity around what she wanted to apply after the programme, the reflective time to engage in action planning created before the end of the programme and the return to the 'real world' made this easier. Thus perhaps in discussing the importance of reflection participants were relating this to action planning as well. Indeed four participants argued that for the development programme to be effective in the long term, time should be built in to managers' jobs to enable them to 'stand back' when necessary. This might take the form of a number of hours each week when they would unavailable for more operational duties. Having said that, most participants (including the four) regarded it as unlikely that such a luxury would be a realistic proposition. Instead, they took what opportunities they could as described above.

Another important factor that seems to have contributed to making time for one's self was the participant's own assertive behaviour. This was reported in four cases, and included being clear about what they wanted to do (for example introduce a change in working methods), and sticking to it. In particular, those who were good at saying 'no' to others when necessary found it less difficult to make the time to reflect. Other participants said they had to work harder at it. Finally, six participants reported that using the autonomy they had in their jobs (and in some cases even realizing they had it) was a critical contributor to increasing their personal capacity for transfer. As one respondent put it, 'Now I think autonomy is there to be taken. I think it is about claiming your autonomy and knowing how much you can claim depending on your level of where you are at.' For those who discussed the issue of autonomy specifically, the culture of the organization in which they worked had not perhaps encouraged autonomy. All participants had at some point in their careers worked in departments and organizations based very much on traditional models of management, where more 'autocratic' styles of management prevailed (Tannenbaum and Schmidt 1973). However, now armed with greater confidence in their role and their ability to perform it (much of this having come from their attendance on the programme), those with higher personal ability to transfer reported being able to influence changes to a greater degree than they thought possible prior to the programme. To take an example, one participant's belief in a particular approach to handling a conflict, reinforced by learning from co-attendees and facilitators, enabled her to withstand pressure from others and persevere with a particular course of action. In summary, the evidence suggests that personal ability to transfer is quite a personal characteristic. Those who demonstrated it to a high level provide strong evidence for a personal responsibility for 'making transfer happen', and the use of one's autonomy, one's peers and one's own time if necessary in order to achieve this.

## Manager Support: The Extent to which Managers and Supervisors Support and Reinforce the Use of Learning on-the-Job

For the participants, the level of manager support varied across organizations. Reports of the level of support ranged from very supportive (seven participants) through to very unsupportive (four participants). The remainder could be regarded as neutral in terms of their level of support. Based primarily on the responses from the former group, but also including observations of other participants interviewed, a 'composite' picture of what a supportive manager looked like in practice is discussed below.

## EMPOWERING MANAGEMENT STYLE

One of the most significant ways in which managers facilitated transfer was through their encouragement and empowerment of the participant, generating a belief in their (the participants) own ability. Critical in this regard was a 'hands off' type of approach (Hersey and Blanchard 1982) that seems to have been so much appreciated by the participants. A high number of them identified in managers who were seen as supportive the fact that 'they let me get on with it.' The following sentiment was echoed several times, 'It suits me. I find it is great to know there is support there if you need it, but yet I don't have someone interfering in the way I would run the department as such.' This is indicative of a more empowering style of management. Participants described it as important from the point of view of maintaining confidence in their own ability to do the job (performance self-efficacy). As already seen, high performance self-efficacy is a factor in transfer outcomes. How this is done is clear enough to see from the evidence. Managers who allowed their staff to perform as they thought appropriate sent a clear message concerning confidence in their ability to do the job. Yet at the same time, being available for support ensured that should the need arise, advice could be sought. The autonomy experienced by the participant allowed them the freedom to take courses of action and make their own decisions, with consequent reported effects for their self-efficacy.

An important component of the 'hands off' style was of course delegation. Supportive managers were not afraid to leave things to individuals. In more specific terms, four participants described behaviour that, while it could sometimes be of a critical nature, was still considered supportive. They discussed the practice in more supportive managers of tending to stand back and adopt a 'coaching' type of role. To quote one respondent, 'I mean she doesn't say, no I think you should do it my way. But what she would say is look, have you thought about the implications for, or how do you think you are going to manage this?'

## PRE-AND POST-PROGRAMME DISCUSSIONS

More specifically related to this development programme and considered important were the pre- and post-programme discussions. These enabled identification of strengths, areas for development, possible applications of learning and so on. Studies cited earlier, in particular Brinkerhoff and Montesino (1995), and Gregoire, Propp and Poertner (1998) support the importance of these activities in facilitating transfer. Amongst supportive managers, this 'loop' was closed following the participants' return from the programme. Typical supportive activity following the programme included a meeting, usually taking place within a week or two. They might use this initial post-programme meeting as a starting point for a coaching process, which could develop into a regular activity. The more supportive managers regularly asked questions, although they weren't slow to give advice when they felt it was needed. In true 'coaching' fashion, such advice would typically be given only after the issues had been explored. As one respondent explained, 'She would talk me through it really, any of the problems I would have and she would relate how she'd handle it herself, a similar situation and she would let me do most of the talking and she'd give me guidance from it.'

## LISTENING AND EMPATHY

It is not surprising therefore that a particular skill reported amongst those supportive managers was listening. It surfaced as an important skill in its own right in many responses. To judge from one response, it seems it should not be taken for granted that this would normally happen, given the culture of obeying and not questioning from which many of the current managers had emerged. One quality of supportive managers perhaps encompassing the above skills is empathy. It was usually cited in a positive sense, but particularly in a small number of cases, lack of empathy was associated with lack of support. Most of the managers regarded as empathetic tended also to be those who were visible and available, many having an 'open door' policy. For example, one participant, describing a past situation, revealed, 'You used to have to ring a bell and there would be a door with 'enter' on it, whereas [name] leaves the door open and people come in and visit all the time.'

## SUPPORTIVE CLIMATE

Availability, empathy, and good listening and questioning skills combine to create a climate of openness, a regularly cited characteristic attributed to supportive managers (Bennett, Lehman and Forst 1999). It was particularly important as a behaviour for facilitating transfer in the context of communication with their staff – taking the form of keeping staff up-to-date with management issues and providing clarity when possible. It was also seen as an important attitude in terms of openness to new learning and ways of doing things. Supportive managers also demonstrated an open style of management with their staff particularly in the areas of involvement of staff in the larger management role, but also in terms of more involvement in meetings, projects and task groups, representing an evolution from a more traditional style. In a broader sense, supportive managers held positive attitudes about the benefits of education and development, as well the need to share them. Such as, 'She herself does presentations to staff in the hospital. She encourages professional development. So as soon as I told her I was on this course she says, "Oh, tell us about it. Come in and talk to us about it and let's see how you can apply this to your job".'

## Peer Support: The Extent to which Peers Reinforce and Support Use of Learning on-the-Job

Some indications regarding the value of peer support have already been seen whilst discussing the importance of networking on the programme. Peers in this case may refer either to co-attendees on the programme or to colleagues at work. As regards colleagues at work, their support manifested itself in different ways. Eight participants reported amongst their peers a general enthusiasm for change, and a willingness to try new ways of doing things. They were interested in what the attendee had learned on the programme. They listened, questioned and openly discussed issues that arose from the training. They gave feedback, both positive and critical, on attempts to put new learning into practice. As described by another respondent, 'So the team here are very open to change and to questioning and going with things, but critically it is a team that can say no or question. I knew when I came back even just changing or introducing ways of doing things I would have positive feedback, which I did.' Support was also demonstrated in other ways (four reports) by peers' willingness to 'plug the gaps' while the participant was away on the programme.

### SUPPORT FROM THE NETWORK

Peer support from fellow attendees came primarily from the network that had been built up around the programme. This was reported by 21 participants. The value to them of that support network, both during and after the programme has already been discussed in the context of action learning and transfer design (Smith and O'Neil 2003). As co-participants on a new learning programme, the residential nature and collegiate style of the programme encouraged support and mutual learning. This was reinforced by the fact that all participants, with wide experience from their current and previous jobs, were able to bring to bear on problems discussed a wealth of expertise from their knowledge of similar situations. There was of course also the practical issue of having contacts in appropriate places in the health service around the country. In summary, therefore, peer support, by its presence or its absence as described here, contributed to the transfer climate by virtue of the cues and consequences (Rouiller and Goldstein 1993; Tracey, Tannenbaum and Kavanagh 1995) regarding the use of training, which have been shown to influence transfer.

## Organizational Climate for Transfer: The Extent to which the Organization as a Whole Supports the Use of Learning on-the-Job

While personal ability to transfer concerns itself primarily with characteristics of the trainee, organization climate, on the other hand, is more about organizational factors. Both, however, reflect the battle with organizational priorities, and the struggle to engage in 'management' rather than 'operational' activity. Organization support was a major issue, discussed specifically by almost all participants, and almost always in the negative sense. It exerted its influence mainly in three different areas. Difficulty in generating opportunities to use learning from the programme was typically brought about by lack of human and other (physical) resources, as well as by structural and industrial relations issues. These factors have already been discussed as barriers to transfer in studies by Newstrom (1986) and Clarke (2002).

### LACK OF HUMAN RESOURCES

As an inhibitor of learning transfer, this issue was cited many times, and discussed in six interviews. Significantly, ongoing financial constraints and increasing job opportunities elsewhere had reduced human resources to the minimum. Consequently, the participants regularly had to leave aside their management role (for which they underwent this development programme) and take on more of an operating role as an ordinary member of the team. To quote an example, 'From a management perspective I am a manager, but I'm also a clinical person. So when I have to look after patients I'm part of the team. So when the department gets busy, that's my management gone skew-ways ... Yesterday it was like Beirut in here so there was nothing done. So now I'm left playing catch-up.'

Lack of human resources also had consequences for the general skills level. Six participants reported that they found themselves unable to implement changes in some areas because of a lack of expertise in certain clinical areas, as well as a lack of administrative support. In addition, they said that releasing staff for appropriate training was sometimes impossible due to the risk of leaving an 'unsafe practice', where particular clinical skills are needed in a particular place at all times. This 'vicious circle' had effects on morale, they suggested, and that in turn this affected absenteeism. 'The staff would inevitably feel, well look if I had a really bad day in there today, this person died ... and I cannot even look at what time my lunch break is going to happen, well I'm going to have a day off. Suddenly then my sickness record is directly affected by how others manage the bigger system.'

## LACK OF OTHER (PHYSICAL) RESOURCES

This too had an important role to play in inhibiting transfer. In some cases, participants referred to technical resources such as IT tools and systems, in other cases financial resources, and in some cases simply equipment that would enable newly learned skills to be put into effect. There was also a sense among some participants, reported in three cases, that perceived lack of organizational support and resources was even an inhibitor to training taking place at all. This happened where numbers were already very tight and training and development activity other than necessary clinical training were continually 'put on the long finger'. Despite the fact that the programme under study was organized and paid for by a central agency rather than the participants' own organizations, this attitude prevailed at those sites.

One way in which participants felt this situation might be alleviated was by having more control over these resources. Six interviewees suggested this could take the form of greater control over training budgets themselves, or at least greater input into training decisions. This, they felt, would allow them to focus on their own priorities, increasing the perceived content validity and thus trainee performance. The practice of the organization arranging the course and then looking for 'bodies' to fill the seats, reported in five different locations would thus be avoided.

## HIERARCHY/STRUCTURE/INDUSTRIAL RELATIONS ISSUES

Another barrier to transferring learning that participants discussed appears to arise from structural issues within their organization itself. It seems that the latitude managers are given to manage depends to some extent on where the 'power' lies within their organization. For eight of the organizations in the study, it was, 'We are dealing with the world of work and people and this is the reality but we still operate in a very medical model culture where what the consultant says goes. I don't mean nurses won't challenge that but the power base is still there.' A smaller number of organizations, however, contrasted sharply with this, being in general newer, smaller and less formal. In both of the cases where the positive effects of organization support were cited, participants emphasized the openness, the lack of bureaucracy, the non-hierarchical climate within the work unit and an ethos that supported development and the sharing of learning. This type of environment has already been identified by Bennett, Lehman and Forst (1999) as conducive to learning transfer. For instance, 'We actually don't work as doctors and nurses. We all do everything. It is probably not the right way even but we work in a sort of place that if something has to be done, it doesn't matter who you are it's done, within reason of course.'

The general level of bureaucracy within the organization appears also to have had an effect on the ability to transfer through interfering with opportunities to use learning. Two particular barriers were cited. In four cases (usually larger, older organizations) it often took inordinate amounts of time to get things done, for example, approval to attend a developmental seminar or visit another organization. In two of these cases, the interviewees sometimes felt that the trouble involved was not going to be worth the effort, and thus didn't pursue some matters with any degree of vigour. As one manager said, 'Hierarchy. The amount of levels it has to go to get even a biro by the looks of it. Red tape, forms that have to be filled in.' Another structural issue arose in an organization that had a sensitive union environment and two participants on the programme. In that situation, some training outcomes were unable to be applied back at work as they would require a small change in the roles of some people involved. While the individuals involved actually welcomed the changes, the union resisted and the change didn't happen. However, such climates did not exist everywhere. Reports of greater flexibility in applying changes brought about by learning came from smaller, more independent (and therefore more autonomous) work units.

## ON THE POSITIVE SIDE

In the more positive examples (admittedly only three cases), the participant's organization took a more active role in integrating training and its application. For instance, in these cases it was reported that they oversaw a process in which participants on the management programme were asked to make presentations about salient parts of the programme to management colleagues. In one case assistance was even given with preparation of the presentation. In another, it was made a condition of attendance that these presentations take place on return from the programme.

## PRE- AND POST-PROGRAMME SUPPORT

A common theme running through the responses focused on the need to integrate the management development programme itself into a larger process that involved pre- and post-programme elements. Some pre-course discussion with the participant's boss was built into the design of the programme, and was intended to take place as part of the participants' competency review. The purpose of the meeting was to look at the programme in the light of the participant's training and development needs, and identify desired training outcomes and post-programme application opportunities. However, it wasn't mandatory, and reports suggest that only about 10 people availed of the opportunity. Those that did reported stronger links between the content of the programme and its application to their own work situation, through better identification of their job priorities and their developmental needs (Baldwin, Magjuka and Loher 1991). Although the programme under study had already been designed without their direct input, they nevertheless felt that such a discussion would be useful for any future developmental opportunities. 'As managers we are going to have to do some kind of needs analysis on everyone, then when training opportunities come up we know who to send, and we'll know who'll get the best out of it. Other people might wonder but we need criteria there for how we are going to do that to be fair to everyone.'

Although such a pre-programme meeting can also be classified as manager support (at an individual level), at an organizational level some of those participants who discussed it felt it should be a formal part of any organizational training and development activity. The effect of providing training without prior needs analysis arose in discussions with the same participants. In the view of some, this meant either that training would be provided that didn't meet any particular needs, or (a greater danger in some views) it created expectations in terms of application that might not be able to be met. For example, 'All you are going to do is frustrate the person even more because you have actually taken them away, taught them how it should work and how it could work and put them back in.' Post-programme, the reality of most situations was that very little emphasis was placed upon what happened after attending the programme. Only four participants (although there were probably more) reported having follow-up meetings with their managers. However, all of these individuals said they found it useful both from the point of view of their manager demonstrating interest, support and coaching, as well as making specific action plans for application of learning.

## SUGGESTIONS FOR IMPROVEMENT

When asked about suggestions for their organization to facilitate the transfer of learning, four participants suggested ways along the lines of those already discussed in which transfer might be improved. As it would seem that organizational support for training such as clinical training was higher (presumably due to a more obvious link between the training and its application), they suggested an extension of the responsibilities of practice development units to deal with management development. Additionally, and more locally, they also recommended the introduction of knowledge sharing sessions and presentations to transfer that knowledge.

In summary, therefore, quite a number of reported organizational conditions affected participants' ability and motivation to transfer learning from the programme. More inhibitors than facilitators were reported, a result reflected in a major early study by Vandenput (1973), and a later one by Clarke (2002). The structure and climate of the work unit were responsible for a number of effects, one of which was to make it more difficult for an individual to make some time to reflect on their learning.

## Learning Outcomes: The Extent to which Participants have Gained New Insights into Themselves and/or Their Role

Transfer of learning was defined in Chapter 2 as the effective and continuing application, by trainees to their jobs, of the knowledge and skills gained in training (Broad and Newstrom 1992). Other reviews of the literature (Ford and Weissbein 1997) point to its multi-faceted nature. One approach to discussion of this multi-faceted nature is that originally put forward by Golembiewski, Billingsley and Jaeger (1976), already discussed. They highlighted the complexity of change in interventions such as the programme in this study, and proposed three types of change that can occur – alpha, beta and gamma change. Based on reports from participants, it appears that all three types of change occurred. For a number of participants, straightforward changes in behaviour at work were also accompanied by deeper levels of change. These changes will shortly be discussed.

With regard to the complex nature of learning and transfer outcomes, a question for this study was whether the function of this management development programme was simply to increase levels of knowledge and skill in particular aspects of management or whether there were other objectives. It will be recalled that in addition to the development of particular leadership and management skills, in terms of both the management of people and the management of financial and other resources, the intended objectives of the programme included:

- the development of an understanding of current trends, innovations and managerial best practice in health service management;

- clarification of their role within the management team;

- the development of a personal development plan to guide their current and ongoing development.

The above suggests that some deeper learning outcomes for the programme were intended. These types of outcomes do not lend themselves easily to measurement other than by personal and often very subjective means. Neither are they included in the competency profile around which the programme was based. However it is precisely these kinds of outcomes that comprise beta changes – changes in participants' rating system of what competency in a particular area entails. This should not be seen as a shortcoming of the programme, however. The programme arose from an important need to develop management capability within the health service, and given that participants' specific role was one that at the time was still evolving, it was quite appropriate that such a programme should seek outcomes that involve deeper questioning and clarification of issues.

## ALPHA CHANGE

This type of change was described as a straightforward variation in the level of knowledge or skill on some dimension along a fixed scale. Improvements in skills, as well as other learning, were reported.

*Improvements in skills* Amongst the 27 participants, 21 reported a straightforward change in their level of one or more management skills. These changes comprised:

- Greater management knowledge. Specific improvements cited (on seven occasions) related to better understanding of the abilities and motivations of their staff.

- More effective meetings. Nine of the participants interviewed expressed the feeling that they now ran their meetings in a more organized fashion, with better outcomes and less time wasted.

- Dealing with conflict better. This was a significantly outcome for many individuals. Twelve participants cited the improvement of their capability in this regard as a key objective in attending the programme. Dealing with conflict better included listening to all sides of a story, not being afraid to take time to reflect on it and sticking by decisions made.

- Greater delegation and empowerment. In all, 13 participants also felt happier that they were now better at delegating work to others.

- Better communication. Six participants reported this as a primary outcome resulting from their attendance on the programme. In some cases it referred to greater meeting effectiveness, but was also related to keeping their staff up-to-date on developments, and providing them with work-related clarity.

- Performance management. Related to improvements in some of the areas just discussed, six participants reported specific improvements in their ability to manage the performance of their staff. Specific improvements cited related to clearer goal setting, giving (and receiving) better quality feedback on performance, coaching and problem solving.

- Time and priority management. Three participants reported making better use of their time.

*Hidden learning*  One other experience, described by two participants as 'hidden' learning, was that some things learned (an example quoted was the successful handling of an interpersonal conflict situation between two staff) did not become apparent (and perhaps even then in an unconscious way) until a long time after the programme. A change such as this would not be likely to show up as a change in competency level after 3 months, and thus has implications for the measurement of changes in competency levels. As one reported, 'It is just sort of there. It is information that you have picked up as a skill. I think every year that you are in a job it becomes easier and easier.'

## BETA CHANGE

Beta change was described as involving some 'recalibration' of the measurement scale, for example where a participant may have reassessed their level of prior knowledge on some dimension in between two measurements. Some of these outcomes will now be discussed.

*Reinforcement* For eight of the participants interviewed, a primary outcome from the programme was simply a reinforcement of what they felt they had been doing as managers all along, but which placed their procedural skills and knowledge in a declarative context. As in, 'I discovered while I was there on that course I actually was doing things right but I suppose I needed somebody to tell me.'

*Understanding competency* According to reports from six participants, participation on the programme allowed them the opportunity to take stock of their understanding of certain competencies of particular relevance to them. As the programme progressed, their understanding of the competencies deepened. 'It's interesting, I would probably have scored myself higher in these prior to going on the course because I did not realize that maybe I had a deficit, but having gone on the course there are areas I have improved on. Maybe improved is not the right word, but I would have thought about differently.'

*Confidence* One thread running through all of the reports of transfer outcomes was that participants now performed their job with greater confidence than before. Ten participants made specific mention of this. They reported that much of this confidence came from the support of a network of managers with similar management issues. Through exposure to a wider range of management problems, they discovered that their own problems weren't unique, or they weren't handling them as badly as they thought – in short, they redefined their level of competency in those areas.

*A more strategic view* Five individuals reported that they now felt they possessed a broader and more strategic view of the role of nurse manager, which helped them in their decision making. 'I would be very conscious of my attitude towards staff, my interaction with staff and how I try to manage staff on a daily basis.'

## GAMMA CHANGE

Finally, gamma change was described in terms of involving a reconceptualization, or a major change in the frame of reference within which phenomena are perceived. An example of such a phenomenon is the participant's role as a manager, and there is evidence in some participant reports that such a reconceptualization of that role and the appropriate skills needed took place. They are discussed below.

*Self insight*  Quite apart from development in the level of specific competencies, 14 participants reported that they learned something new about themselves, their style, their strengths and their weaknesses. Many of these cited the use of instruments such as the Myers Briggs Type Indicator and the competency profile as being very helpful in making them think more deeply about their preferences, their capabilities, their developmental needs and even their career options.

*Clarity of role*  Related to the above were the responses of a further five participants that much-needed clarity surrounding their role as a nurse manager had been found. Clarification had the effect of increasing their motivation to perform the role, or in the case of one individual, to move out of the role and into another area of work within the profession. 'That has made me think really in the last 6 months, where do I want to go, do I want to stay in management all my life, or go back to the clinical area and work forward that way?'

*Opening minds and broadening horizons*  A further outcome reported by four participants was the fact that in some perhaps intangible way, attendance at the programme had 'opened their minds' or 'broadened their horizons'. Broadening horizons for some of them was understanding more about their own role and its responsibilities, or broadening their knowledge of the range of issues that are pertinent to health service managers everywhere, or placing a context around much of their management tasks. When they spoke of 'opening minds', they referred to the same things, along with a greater understanding of the strengths and weaknesses of others.

*A new approach to managing*   In all, four participants stated categorically that they had found a 'new approach to managing', citing the combination of new skills, competencies and insights afforded by their attendance at the programme. 'So therefore I am looking at things in a completely different way.'

## Acknowledgement

The author would like to thank those participants who gave so generously of their time to be interviewed for the above study.

## References

Baldwin, T.T., Magjuka, R.J. and Loher, B.T. (1991). The perils of participation: Effects of choice of training on trainee motivation and learning. *Personnel Psychology*, 44, 51–65.

Bennett, J.B., Lehman, W.E.K. and Forst, J.K. (1999). Change, transfer climate and customer orientation: A contextual model and analysis of change-driven training. *Group and Organization Management*, 24, 188–216.

Brinkerhoff, R.O. and Montesino, M.U. (1995). Partnerships for training transfer: Lessons from a corporate study. *Human Resource Development Quarterly*, 6, 263–74.

Broad, M.L. and Newstrom, J. (1992). *Transfer of training: Action-packed strategies to ensure high payoff from training investments.* New York: Addison Wesley.

Brown, T.C. and Latham, G.P. (2000). The effects of goal setting and self-instruction training on the performance of unionized employees. *Relations Industrielles*, 55(1), 80–95.

Burke, L.A. (1997). Improving positive transfer: A test of relapse prevention training on transfer outcomes. *Human Resource Development Quarterly*, 8(2), 115–28.

Carlson, D.S., Bozeman, D.P., Kacmar, K.M. Wright, P.M. and McMahan,G.C. (2000). Training motivation in organizations: An analysis of individual-level antecedents. *Journal of Managerial Issues*, 12(3), 271–87.

Clark, R.E. (1990, April). A cognitive theory of instructional method. Paper presented at the Annual Meeting of the American Educational Research Association, Boston, MA.

Clarke, N. (2002). Job/work environment factors influencing training transfer within a human service agency: Some indicative support for Baldwin and Ford's transfer climate construct. *International Journal of Training & Development*, 6(3), 146–62.

Colquitt, J.A., LePine, J.R. and Noe, R.A. (2000). Trainee attributes and attitudes revisited: A meta-analysis of research on training motivation. *Journal of Applied Psychology*, 85(5), 678–707.

Facteau, J.D., Dobbins, G.H., Russell, J.E.A., Ladd, R.T. and Kudisch, J.D. (1995). The influence of general perceptions of the training environment on pretraining motivation and perceived training transfer. *Journal of Management*, 21, 1–25.

Ford, J.K. and Weissbein, D.A. (1997). Transfer of training: An updated review and analysis. *Performance Improvement Quarterly*, 10(2), 22–41.

Golembiewski, R.T., Billingsley, K. and Jaeger, S. (1976). Measuring change and persistence in human affairs. *Journal of Applied Behavioral Science*, 12, 133–57.

Gregoire, T.K., Propp, J., and Poertner, J. (1998). The supervisor's role in the transfer of training. *Administration in Social Work*, 22(1), 1–18.

Hersey, P. and Blanchard, K.L. (1982). *Management of organizational behavior: Utilizing human resources. 4th ed.* Englewood Cliffs, NJ; Prentice-Hall.

Hicks, W.D. and Klimowski, R.J. (1987). Entry into training programs and its effects on training outcomes: A field experiment. *Academy of Management Journal*, 30, 542–52.

Jennings, D. (2002). Strategic management: An evaluation of the use of three learning methods. *The Journal of Management Development*, 21(9/10), 655–65.

MacDonald, C.J., Gabriel, M.A. and Cousins, J.B. (2000). Factors influencing adult learning in technology based firms. *The Journal of Management Development*, 19, 220–40.

Magjuka, R., Baldwin, T.T. and Loher, B.T. (1994). The combined effects of three pretraining strategies on motivation and performance: An empirical exploration. *Journal of Managerial Issues*, 6(3), 282–296.

Marsick, V.J. and O'Neil, J. (1999). The many faces of action learning. *Management Learning*, 30(2), 159–76.

Naylor, J.C. and Briggs, G.E. (1983). The effect of task complexity and task organization on the relative efficiency of part and whole training methods. *Journal of Experimental Psychology*, 65, 217–24.

Newstrom, J.W. (1986). Leveraging management development through the management of transfer. *Journal of Management Development*, 5, 33–45.

Peters, T. (1987). *Thriving on chaos: Handbook for a management revolution.* London: Macmillan.

Peters, L.H. and O'Connor, E.J. (1980). Situational constraints and work outcomes: The influences of a frequently overlooked construct. *Academy of Management Review*, 5, 391–98.

Quinones, M.A. and Ehrenstein, A. (eds.), (1996). *Training for a rapidly changing workplace: Applications of psychological research.* Washington, DC: American Psychological Association.

Rouiller, J.Z. and Goldstein, I.L. (1993). The relationship between organizational transfer climate and positive transfer of training. *Human Resource Development Quarterly*, 4, 377–90.

Seale, C. (1999). *The quality of qualitative research.* London: Sage.

Sloan, E.B. (2001). *The contribution of university-based executive education to corporate executive talent management results.* Joint research project conducted by the international university consortium for executive education (UNICON) and Personnel Decisions International. Minneapolis: Personnel Decisions International. In K. Kraiger (ed.), *Creating, implementing, and managing effective training and development: State-of-the-art lessons for practice.* San Francisco: Jossey-Bass.

Smith, P.A. and O'Neil, J. (2003). A review of action learning literature 1994–2000: Part 2 – signposts into the literature. *Journal of Workplace Learning,* 15(4), 154–66.

Smith, P.L. and Ragan, T.J. (1993). *Instructional design.* New York: Macmillan. In Z. Yildirim, M.Y. Ozden, and M. Aksu (2001), Comparison of hypermedia learning and traditional instruction on knowledge acquisition and retention. *The Journal of Educational Research,* 94(4), 207–20.

Stevens, C.K. and Gist, M.E. (1997). Effects of self efficacy and goal-orientation training on interpersonal skill maintenance: What are the mechanisms? *Personnel Psychology,* 50(4), 955–78.

Tannenbaum, R. and Schmidt, W.H. (1973). How to choose a leadership pattern. *Harvard Business Review,* 51, 166–68.

Tesluk, P.E., Farr, J.L. Mathieu, J.E. and Vance, R.J. (1995). Generalization of employee involvement training to the job setting: Individual and situational effects. *Personnel Psychology,* 48, 607–32.

Tracey, J.B. Tannenbaum, S.I. and Kavanagh, M.J. (1995). Applying trained skills on the job: The importance of the work environment. *Journal of Applied Psychology,* 80, 239–52.

Vandenput, M.A.E. (1973). The transfer of learning: Some organizational variables. *Journal of European Training,* 2, 251–62.

# Index